PENGU

Miran

Denis Edwards was born and bred in Miramar, Wellington. He is one of a family of six children. Educated at Holy Cross, Marist Miramar primary schools and later St Patrick's College, he went from school to the New Zealand Police, serving as a cadet and constable for three years.

Denis Edwards worked for nine years as a paramedic and dispatcher for the St John Ambulance Association before turning an interest in writing into a career.

He has written for almost every magazine and newspaper in New Zealand and for newspapers in Australia and England. He has been a finalist in the New Zealand Sports Journalist Awards and the Qantas Press Awards. *Miramar Dog* is his fourth book. *Vows; priests and nuns speak out* was also published by Penguin. *Eden* was published by Time Capsule Publishing. *Killer Moves* is published by Scholastic.

He lives in Auckland's Mount Eden, close to the cafes and some distance from the Mount Eden Prison.

Author photo Keith Scott

miramar DOG

Denis Edwards

PENGUIN BOOKS

PENGUIN BOOKS

Penguin Books (NZ) Ltd, cnr Airborne and Rosedale Roads, Albany,
Auckland 1310, New Zealand
Penguin Books Ltd, 27 Wrights Lane, London W8 5TZ, England
Penguin USA, 375 Hudson Street, New York, NY 10014, United States
Penguin Books Australia Ltd, 487 Maroondah Highway, Ringwood,
Australia 3134
Penguin Books Canada Ltd, 10 Alcorn Avenue, Toronto, Ontaria,
Canada M4V 3B2

Penguin Books Ltd, Registered Offices: Harmondsworth, Middlesex,
England

First published by Penguin Books (NZ) Ltd, 1998

1 3 5 7 9 10 8 6 4 2

Copyright © Denis Edwards 1998

Designed & typeset by Benedict Reid at Egan Reid Ltd
Printed in Australia by Australian Print Group, Maryborough

To
John and Jane
My long-suffering and ever-tolerant younger brother
and sister

CATHOLIC DOG
SITTING ON A LOG
EATING A BELLY
OUT OF A FROG
Popular taunting rhyme, Miramar circa 1950

introduction

I'm Denis. I'm eight and this
is my story, and the story of my family and some of the
people around us. It is set when I was eight because
that was when many of the things described in this book
happened. Some of the other things, particularly the
effects of Frank Wilkins' visit to the Newtown
workshop to explain his accounting, and what
happened to him there and afterwards, happened
earlier. So did the aftermath of the sermon; the arsonist,

the lawyers, the wives, the nuns, the priests and the violinist, and the desperate effort to save Catholic men from perdition and ruin. The slygrogs, the morning talks and the experiment with the media all happened more or less at the same time as the soccer match.

Our family was near the centre of all this. It had been in Wellington since the 1930s, not long enough or rich or influential enough to be a Great Family. But long enough to be close to the currents diverted from the main stream and flowing in unpredictable directions.

My grandfather had shifted the family to Wellington. He had tired of being the policeman at Takaka, near Nelson, and having to fight the drunken concrete workers every Saturday night. Once across Cook Strait he would end his working life as a warder at Mount Crawford prison. He was the oldest man working there, and because he was a kindly soul he wound up being given the job of sitting up at night with the condemned men. He would wait with them through their last night, until 8am, when they would be executed on the prison gallows.

He would leave them at seven, and walk down to the house at 144 Nevay Road. On those days breakfast was a silent affair, until the prison siren sounded at precisely eight o'clock, the signal the hanging was happening.

There was one man who had sat and talked through the night, most of it cleaning away a life spent in the courts, prison and doing harm to other people and their possessions. At seven, when my grandfather was due to leave, the man looked him right in the eye and said in a calm voice, 'I didn't do it. I never killed her.'

That day the silence over breakfast lasted until nightfall. My grandfather took the edge off hearing the dead man's denial with a whisky binge.

The unofficial history of Miramar, and of Wellington, spun and bounced off the walls of our house, mostly in the little room just beside our kitchen. The back door opened into it and was the door everyone used at our house. It was the best way to approach, because you could see the Wellington Harbour and the boats, or the foaming waves or the cold steel-grey of the water just before the storm arrived, or when it was calm and the sea was soft green or blue.

In 1968 we stood outside that room, and watched the inter-island ferry, *Wahine*, drag itself up the harbour, to stop opposite Seatoun and slowly roll on its side, and we saw the clouds of steam rising hundreds of feet in the air. The water had run down its funnels and into the boilers. When that happened the ship could not be saved. My father sobbed when he saw that. He had been at sea, on ships like the *Wahine*, and for him its loss was a death.

That little dining room was where I heard a lot of things, many of them from my father and his friends when they were drinking together, slowly emptying the warm beer from the flagons, drinking from peanut butter glasses. They gradually ceased to care about the little kids wandering around. They kept telling their stories and passing on their gossip, forgetting that little kids remember things.

There was a lot to remember. Our family was mixed up in almost everything in Wellington, except banking and big business. Uncle Dennis was near the heart of the Labour Party and on the Petone Borough Council. My father and mother were heavily involved in Catholic affairs, which meant news of strange things and fears and excitement came through our house, borne by a procession of Marists, Franciscans, Dominicans, Redemptorists and Sisters of Mercy.

To be deep in Catholic affairs was to be just a short jump from the union movement, and from there to the radicals fighting to keep hard-won pay and conditions. Toby Hill, who was the second-in-command of the Watersiders Union during the bitter lockout in 1951, when people talked about civil war, when terrible legislation was shoved through Parliament making it illegal to give food or other help to watersiders, would come to our house. Mostly it was because his wife and my mother were friends. They had much in common, mostly the struggle with raising children with too little money.

Friends of my grandfather visited. Some were still in the police or working in the prison, or were retired, but they knew the stories, and as the beer and food appeared they relaxed and talked of strange people, strange events, and awful deaths.

This means that some of the stories, repeated here, are second-hand, verified as best I can by talking to the people still living, adding weight and substance to the fragments I already knew. As I got older and the people who are the focus of these stories died, and could no longer be hurt and offended, people would feel able to open up and tell me the choices they faced and the things they had done.

Some people's names have been changed. Some are still alive and might not want their story told. Other names have been changed because while the people are dead, their children are still alive. They might want to tell their story their way. My name, those of my parents and brothers and sister are real. The rest have been changed. Readers will notice a gap in the time line. Frank Wilkins and Marie West died in 1947. The rest of the story, of our family, and the events leading up to the soccer match, the effective end of the Catholic ghetto in Miramar, takes place a few years later. This has not affected the story, simply removed the need to fill in the intervening years, when little of relevance happened.

Most of the people at the heart of the story came through our house. When my mother and father married, Pat Conlin sat at a table near the front of the room. Uncle Pat was important. He was Wellington's most important bookmaker. The legend was he had been working in the South Island, where my grandfather was born. There was a suggestion he was my grandfather's half-brother, but we never really found out for sure.

Pat had been working in Christchurch. There had been a strike. The employers brought in strike-breakers. Pat helped some of them rethink their commitment to the employers, with a piece of four by two timber. At least one man was never quite the same after Pat finished using his head as a drum. Pat got four years in prison for that, and did four, when he could have done three, because of a couple of incidents with prison officers, for which he paid with long sessions in the punishment wing.

Pat emerged into an employment market then screaming for anyone upright and with a pulse, but could not find work. His reputation was too fearsome, and employers kept blacklists. He drifted to Wellington, struggling along on bits and pieces of work. When his fourth child arrived he decided enough was enough. Prodded by an anxious wife, he set out to make some money.

It was just after two on a Saturday afternoon when he walked into Arthur Cody's slygrog and bookmaking set-up and told Arthur that he was now a partner in the business.

Arthur looked at him through his rheumy old eyes. 'Why don't ya fuck off, before ya get taught a few fuckin' manners!'

Pat kicked Arthur in the balls. Arthur gasped and spluttered for Alex, his standover man, to kill Pat. He was disappointed at what happened next. What happened next was absolutely nothing. Alex and Pat had been in Paparua prison together. The afternoon before they had shared a jug of beer in the Caledonian Hotel, and Alex had suggested the gaming industry as a career. Pat liked the idea.

Arthur Cody, rolling around on the floor with his hands over his groin, looked up at the two men. It was not difficult to work out what was going on. He took one hand away from his balls and held it up in the air. Pat shook hands with Arthur.

Not long after this Arthur Cody took the suitcase full of banknotes from under his floorboards and retired from the industry. Pat went on to bring a considerable energy and imagination to the work, tripling the turnover and creating jobs and opportunities, and behind them, no small amount of misery, because his debt-collecting policy was to commence with aggression and violence and escalate from there.

His success caught the eye of the man who would be sitting at the same table, enjoying my parents' wedding reception. Murray McCarthy was famous for being the toughest of the tough policemen. A lot of rumours curled in the air around him. One story had him beating a suspect to death. Another, more closely based on fact, was his taking a very mature attitude to certain activities. One of these was bookmaking. McCarthy took the view that people did not have to bet. If they lost it was their own fault and they could expect consequences.

It was not long before Pat Conlin and Murray McCarthy's career paths intersected, and they quickly reached an understanding. Conlin would arrange for people to be available for bookmaking arrests, to enhance the police reputation for diligence in the war on illegal gambling.

Soon after, McCarthy's standard of living began improving. He bought a better car and his wife and children were much better dressed. Mentioning this was not considered wise. One man did. Not long afterwards his car was found to be full of stolen property when stopped by the police.

McCarthy kept the Wellington police's Homo Register. These were the files on sexually active homosexuals. In those days any homosexual act, anywhere and by anyone, was illegal. McCarthy expanded the definition of 'homo' to include any sex offender. Anyone caught stealing women's underwear, flashing his penis anywhere except at a urinal or in a rugby dressing shed, who interfered with children, had sex with carnies—unlawful carnal knowledge of a girl under sixteen—or who spent too much time around the Courtenay Place public toilets known as the Taj Mahal, because it resembled a small version of the great building in India, left behind as an architectural joke by a team of long-gone city engineers and architects. All these people were classified as 'homos' and became citizens of a world ruled by Murray McCarthy.

From there on, until they died, they would be harassed. They could expect to be stopped whenever there was a sex crime. They would have to prove their whereabouts when the crime happened, or they would be taken down to Wellington Central and given time to explain themselves. If they did not co-operate they would be visited at work. Nervous employers would find reasons to move them on. If they complained it was taken as proof they had something to hide, and grounds for freshening up their entry in the Homo Register, so they would be stopped more often.

My mum never liked Murray McCarthy much. There was too much of a sense of darkness around him. She was sure his years of roaming around the ugly side of people's lives had left him cynical, angry and slightly prone to depressive fits when he was capable of hurting people, to make himself feel better by comparison.

Much of this story is written in direct quotes. I was there, or the conversations were told to me by my mother or father, or by one of the people involved. I take the view that if you know half a conversation and there is a subsequent action, as happened in the little saga of the two priests, then it is reasonable to fill in the gaps even if I wasn't there.

Conversations where I was not there, and did not speak to the participants, but where I know what happened after their conversation, I have reconstructed and shown without quotation marks.

Some of the story flowed through the confessional, let slip after the priests had spoken of strange events without actually mentioning names — and sometimes letting things slip, knowing the person was dead and could not be betrayed.

There were others who had an interest in muddying the trail. Mick Mahon was one. He had worked with my grandfather, had liked and respected him, and kept in contact with our family. Mahon, a devout Catholic, had talent and had risen in the police to become an inspector. Once he had crossed into the ranks of the commissioned officers he was able to do more or less as he wished. One of the things he wished was to spend hours talking to the police librarian, a man often denigrated for not being out on the front lines, like a 'proper' policeman.

Mahon was different. He was interested and was kind and treated the librarian with dignity. In return the librarian taught him the quiet little pathways through the files, including the built-in checks and double checks to prevent files going missing.

After the librarian went home Mahon would come back to the library and spend long hours, looking for and finding what he wanted. He was a modest man, who knew he had achieved a great deal, and none of it would earn him medals or commendations. He did not worry and he did not say much. He just smiled his queer little smile, watched through his soft lazy eyes as the Freemasons, his mortal enemies in the police, foundered when digging in the files for information on prominent Catholics.

All this — crime, politics and Catholics versus Freemasons, then a bitter and real rivalry — was talked about, argued over and raged at in our house in Nevay Road. Not that I cared. I had other things on my mind. One of them was being fed up at the way the cricket season had ended. Kilbirnie, who became the eastern suburbs representatives in the Wellington-wide finals, had just beaten our under-10 Marist Miramar cricket team. Kilbirnie lost to Karori, who would be plastered by Johnsonville in the finals. It did not look as if we would have had much chance anyway, but this did not matter. We played to win.

Now the soccer season is beginning. Teams have been selected and are under way. There is a lot of soccer. Games are on both Wednesday and Saturday. This makes it more attractive than rugby, the national religion. It offers only one game a week. Those who want to play all the time choose soccer.

The mothers promote soccer. They don't like rugby's inherent violence. Headmasters dedicated to rugby have long, intense sessions with the parents, especially the mothers, and especially after a game produces injuries. These headmasters always provided themselves with an escape route, a soccer team.

The eight and nine-year-olds in our team, playing in the the Under-11 grade, but which through a quirk of eligible birthdays excludes ten-year-olds, have done their calculations. The wisdom at the start of the season was that if the Marist Miramar team could win the easy games against Seatoun, Strathmore, Kilbirnie and Lyall Bay and Miramar South, and got a draw against Miramar Central, and hopefully another one against the consistently best team, Miramar North, we had a chance of winning the league.

Winning matters. There is a religious component to boasting — losers are jeered and taunted as failures, and it is pointed out which religious affiliation, Catholic or Protestant, is superior.

Of course the same calculations are being made at the Protestant schools, where eight and nine-year-olds are also pondering the consequences of losses, and particularly at losing to a mob of Catholics.

Powerful passions surge and roll around Miramar and are about to be let loose.

chapter one

It turned out to be surprisingly easy to do serious damage to another person. Killing them was also a lot quicker than the usual ritual, which took nearly an hour of yelling, threatening, kicking and punching in the balls, stomach, ribs and face, particularly the nose. For most of the time the person at the centre of this attention was lying on the ground, begging for the punishment to stop, and yes, they would swear they would be more diligent about settling their accounts. It was an almost-civilised routine, with a definite script. Pat Conlin sometimes thought its air of ceremony resembled the Catholic Mass: everyone knew how it would start, what would happen in the middle and how it would end. Until now no one had ever been killed in these sessions. Damaged past the point of repair, certainly. But killed? No.

Joe was looking at Pat, who was staring open-mouthed at Frank Wilkins lying there on the floor. This was well past the Mass. This was real. Joe had felt the rush of red mist when Frank began his lying and cracking jokes about the trouble he had caused by not paying off his winners. The instant that sneering grin spread across his face Joe had decided to teach him a real lesson, grabbing the ball peen hammer, swinging it high and then down. It was still picking up speed and force as it smashed into Frank's big, bald head.

Whuuump! Just one smooth movement, and then that soft, folding sound, like punching a feather pillow. Now Frank was on the floor, his suit stained with the oil dropping on the floor from the machines in the workshop. No one was worried about that. Frank wore cheap suits and he had never looked after them properly.

For Joe it was the eyes that were the most shocking. They looked straight up, not seeing anything, a spooky stare like the eels in the fish shop window. He was also surprised. He thought there would be blood and brains all over the place. But no. The hammer had gone into Frank's skull, which didn't seem to be much tougher than the piecrusts his wife baked. That might not be fair. His wife made these incredibly tough piecrusts, and her pies were almost impossible to eat.

He pulled the hammer out of Frank's skull. It had little bits of blue and red sticking to its business end. Jesus! Those were Frank's brains. He dropped the hammer on the floor, shuddering at the sight. Frank was twitching and fitting. White spittle and blood were coming out of his mouth and his legs were flicking up and down and back and forward. It looked horrible.

Pat had recovered enough to yell at him. — Joe, you fucking stupid prick! You've fucking topped him off.

This was not quite correct. Frank's twitching and fitting were signs of some sort of life. There was more blood than spittle dribbling out of his mouth.

— What'd you bloody do that for? Pat half-screeched.

— Cause the bastard started giving cheek again, and we're not here to put up with that. Joe's voice was high, panicky. He could not take his eyes off the ghastly sight on the floor that was spraying a fine, bloody mist over his immaculately polished shoes.

— Look at him! I've seen dogs doing that. Maybe we could drop him off down at the hospital, Joe blurted out, still wide-eyed with revulsion.

Pat was trying to keep thinking through this. — Joe lad, don't be fuckin' stupid. The bloody nurses'll be straight on to the coppers, who'll be round here in about two minutes.

— Maybe it'll be one of our coppers. Flick 'em a few quid to fuck off. Joe's fear was losing the battle with sense and logic.

Pat took a breath. His problem was no longer Frank. It was Joe. — This is murder, he said. — Our coppers won't help with this. Taking ten quid a week to keep away from a few bookies in pubs is a bit bloody different. Shit, this'd be their first murder this year. There'll be dozens of them all over this. Trust me, at least one of them will want to crack the case.

Pat had tried but his years of controlling people through sarcasm had been too much for him. Joe was turning pitiful. — Don't talk to me like I'm a dumb bastard. I'm not going to the Mount (Crawford prison) and I'm not swinging. I'm gonna put him out of his misery.

Joe was first to the desk drawer, and the huge .45 revolver. — Don't shoot him! Pat yelled.

Too late. Joe was holding the gun in both hands, closing his eyes as he pointed it at the man on the floor.

Pat waved his arm. — Joe! There's still a chance. We can drop him in the streets where he'll get found.

Too late. Joe had pulled back the revolver's hammer and fired. Pat bounced back from the force of the explosion in such a confined space. Joe fired again, and again, and again.

Pat propped himself against the wall, trying to keep control. Joe had gone nuts. Panicking about killing someone and now he was finishing the job. Didn't anything make sense?

Joe was still pulling the trigger. The gun was clicking on the empty chambers. Pat gasped. — Well, it's sure as hell a murder now.

Joe dropped the revolver beside the hammer. Pat

grabbed it before Joe could remember where the extra bullets were kept.

Pat bent over Frank. His chest was still moving! He held his hand over the man's mouth. He felt a faint stream of air being sucked in and exhaled. — Amazing! He's still alive!

Pat put the gun in his pocket. He didn't want Joe getting it off him and starting all over again. He eased Joe into a chair, waving at him to just sit still and try to calm down.

Pat was beginning to get angry. Why did he have to solve all the problems? Why couldn't some of these guys sort out their own messes? He was sick of being a mother to these stupid fools, especially when they went bananas and did something like this. At least there was one good thing. Frank had stopped that horrible twitching, although the blood around his mouth was making little bubbles as his irregular gasps of breath went through it.

Three hours later Pat Conlin was shutting his eyes and doing some breathing of his own. He pulled the sea air deep into his nostrils. It looked as if it was going to be all right. He had been able to keep Joe more or less calm for the last three hours. They'd hefted Frank into the boot of his car and driven him from the workshop in Newtown to the Miramar wharf and slid him into the harbour. It was an outgoing tide. He would be on his way out to the heads and then into Cook Strait. From there it was the Tasman Sea and the sharks.

Pat fingered the gun in his pocket. It was loaded now. The plan was for Joe to follow Frank into the drink. But when it came time Pat just couldn't bring himself to haul it out and blast the fool into the next life. He had remembered Joe's wife and teenage daughters up in Hawker Street, on Mount Victoria. So that was the end of that. They didn't deserve him, but he was all they had.

Joe and Pat made sure there were no piles of brains or anything in the boot of Frank's car, and drove it back to Marjoribanks Street, not far from Hawker Street. Both went home to their families and a decent home-cooked dinner.

Two days later Pat did not want his dinner, or anything else to eat, which was unusual for him. Frank Wilkins had been found. The radio news was saying he had been fished out of Evans Bay. A retired carrier had seen the body floating on the surface, forgot about his morning constitutional and called the police, who pulled the body into a little boat. They took it into town, to the post-mortem table, where it was sliced, cut and probed. Amazed doctors told the police they had never seen anything like it. Frank had five bullets, plus the head injury. He had been alive when he went into the water, although probably unconscious. He had drowned!

An *Evening Post* reporter found out that Frank had been alive when he went into the harbour. It was front page. Pat shook his head. This was the worst possible news. It added extra sensation to the case, and would make the coppers doubly determined to produce an offender.

Policemen tracked down Frank's friends and business associates. Most of the latter left Wellington. The former were very keen to tell the police exactly where those associates could be located.

It was not a good time for Pat Conlin. The police wanted answers, preferably from someone who would be hanging in front of official witnesses at Mount Crawford prison. In between sessions in quiet rooms at Wellington Central, handcuffed to a chair and having his head bashed by policemen wielding telephone books, Pat Conlin was a worried man, giving a lot of thought to his future.

chapter two

Colleen Edwards, my mum, is standing in our kitchen, looking at her husband Kevin. He's my dad. It is half past one on a Saturday afternoon. Dad is just back from being over the road helping Jim Graham prune his Chinese gooseberry bush. Their pruning technique is different. No one would ever find it in the *Yates Garden Guide*, or in any other gardening book for that matter. They don't bother with ladders or looking for new or old growth or anything like that, and they don't have pruning shears either. Instead they set up a flagon of Red Band beer and a couple of glasses and sit on the balcony overlooking the garden. They have a few glasses each, but not too many, because they are going to need to see straight when they begin the pruning.

They exchange news. Or rather Jim Graham does. 'Fucking wharfies are playing up again. Bloody smoke money this time, and they're going on about overtime payments again. Bastards.'

Jim works for the Waterfront Industries Commission, which oversees the Wellington wharves and which more or less permanently feels it is held to ransom by the demands of the Waterside Workers Union.

'Dunno the answer to that, Jim.'

'Bastards!'

Once this is out of the way Jim sidles off to the closet. His wife Leah says, 'No, you aren't.'

'Of course I am. It's all right!'

'Where are Michael and Daniel?'

'They're at football. There's no problem.'

'Huh!' she says, unconvinced, and bends back to cutting fabric for the wedding dresses she makes and fits from home.

Jim reaches around in the closet until he finds the air rifle. He gets the pellets from the basement and joins my father on the balcony. Another couple of beers go down the hatches.

Then they take turns at shooting at the old growth on the Chinese gooseberry vine, pruning it away when they score a hit. They have a rough ratio of eight shots per success. On an average Saturday they could get through a box of three hundred pellets, a lot of cheerfully bad language, a flagon of Red Band beer, a bottle of Waikato, which draws a 'Sorry Kev, I don't know how this crap got into the house, so let's get rid of it quickly', a pot of tea and some scones.

There has only been one disaster. One day last year, Ma Dayton from three houses down is looking for her cat, tiptoeing behind the Chinese gooseberry. She gets shot in the back and lets out a scream. Things start happening quickly after that. The cat disappears the instant she lets out her formidably high-pitched scream. She has also spotted my dad and Jim Graham, so they have to go to her aid.

Jack Dayton is running over, because he has heard the scream and is hoping that she might have finally met her Maker. Phone calls are made. Doctor Thompson's surgery is still open. Yes, he'll wait until she turns up.

She's howling about permanent damage to her spinal cord. No one can find a wound, entrance or exit or anything. But she keeps screaming and complaining, so she gets a trip to the doctor.

Jack helps her into the car. As he goes back round to the driver's seat he passes my dad and Jim Graham. They are white-faced and embarrassed and apologising. Jack slaps them on the back. 'Don't worry. She'll be all right. She's as tough as old boots. Take more than that to slow her down. Now if you'd used a .303 or a .22 you might have done some proper damage. But you did the best you could!'

'Start the car, Jack. I might be dying for all I know,' she cries.

'Yes dear,' Jack mutters, and they drive off.

She does not go to hospital. Doctor Thompson looks after her and sends her back home. She tells Mrs Bacon about her adventure. Mrs Bacon has a cup of tea with Mrs Townsend, who tells Leah Graham, who tells my Mum, who joins the rest in being sworn to secrecy.

Ma Dayton is excited. She is beginning to see her experience as a wonderful adventure. She is especially keen on her husband's reaction. So far he has not called her stupid, told her to 'put a sock in it' or muttered about giving her a clip round the ear. It is all she needs to convince herself he is still in love with her. That night, while he's asleep, she rewards him by swinging herself over him. Before he realises what is happening she has fumbled around in his pyjama pants, freed his cock and is on top of him, having sex, the first since her birthday.

She gets that feeling, which she thinks might just be an orgasm. Jack doesn't have one. He's too scared, watching her rock back and forward, in wilder and wilder gyrations. He's frightened that she'll break his prick in half, and he needs it in good working order. He is a salesman, making stops at shops all round the lower North Island. In Bulls, Taumarunui, Te Kuiti, Shannon, Carterton, Greytown and Martinborough his shops are run by women who love to see him. Jack Dayton's arrival is the cue for the 'Back in Ten Minutes' sign to go on the door, and stay there for a good hour or more.

As she leaps around on top of him Jack remembers

that this is a woman who has been shot. Now she is going berserk. What happens if the Doc got it wrong and she dies while they are locked together? If she rolls off he can forget earning a living. Ma Dayton sees the raw terror in his eyes, assumes he is getting the feeling too, and goes faster, enjoying her 'feeling', only her third in eighteen years of married life.

This year it is all okay. Dad and Jim Graham check to make sure Ma Dayton and her new cat are somewhere else. They enjoy a morning's pruning. Dad is now thinking this is a good time to get out on the harbour, toss a line over the side of his dinghy and come home with some nice fish.

There is a ritual to be gone through first. Dad speaks first. 'We're all right here now. I thought I might get away, get a couple of fish for dinner.'

Mum is in the kitchen, the setting for this little play. She looks around to see which of the boys has been the most irritable, cabin-fevered and grizzly. It's me. 'Take Denis with you. He needs to get out of the place a bit.'

'I was thinking of just getting out for a bit, on my own.'

'No. Take Denis with you!'

'But he looks all right there. He'll get a soccer game going with some of the kids.'

Mum looks out the kitchen window. 'It doesn't look as if it is going to rain. It might be a good chance to get on to the lawns. They are getting a bit long.'

Dad looks around. 'Denis! We are going out.'

I appear from my room where I have been hiding

out, grumpily wondering what to do with the rest of the afternoon.

'Where are we going? Are we going to the Basin Reserve to see Marist playing Miramar Rangers? It'll be a good game.'

'No, we're going fishing.'

'What about going to the Basin Reserve?'

This is complicated. Diplomacy is required, or no one will get what they want. Dad could be stuck here. Mum, already plagued by a restless child, gets a moping husband, who knows the steep lawns are there and that the hand mower is waiting under the house.

We all look at each other. Who will break first?

Mum always does. 'Denis, you can play soccer down at Miramar Park tomorrow.' That's me taken care of.

'You can take him down there!' That's my father being offered a deal—take Denis fishing and I'll overlook it when you renege on taking Denis to Miramar Park tomorrow. He nods. He'll take it.

I don't know. Dad doesn't look completely happy. Getting stuck out on the harbour might not be fun. I look up at Mum. If I mess this up I'm next in line for lawnmowing duty. I look back and forward between them. Fishing or lawnmowing. Lawnmowing or fishing. Take fishing. It might get better because Dad always smuggles a couple of quart bottles of beer out with him. He relaxes after he has them.

Everyone nods. The little ritual is over. Dad is off to get his fishing stuff. I get my jersey and wait by the road, leaning on the car in case he forgets to take me. This has happened before.

Besides, last time we went we didn't catch any fish, so I didn't have to listen to any lectures on how good he is at catching them. I bet we don't see any fish.

chapter three

I am the first to see the three fish. One is just ahead of the other two. They are all about two and a half feet long, all flickering silver, blue and pink in the water. Their tails barely move as they race to and then under the boat, aiming towards the harbour entrance.

They are beautiful; elegant, unconcerned, perfect and at home. For just a moment, looking at them and their background of a blue sky, a few fluffy white clouds and the dark green of the Miramar North and Seatoun Heights hills, dotted with the houses clinging to the slopes, it is a moment of the world at its best.

'Oh shit. Quick. Get a line in the water!'

My father had also seen the fish. His view is different. These are dinners getting away. It is too late. They have gone. He shrugs and has a wry smile. There is no need to worry too much. He has four wet snapper in the damp sack lying in the bottom of the boat. There is an occasional jerk from the sack as the fish flip their tails, trying to swim away from this dark jail. Over the afternoon these twitches have been fewer and fewer as the fish exhaust themselves in their smelly sacking.

Dad sits back in the stern of the little dinghy. 'Isn't this good, son? It's not like this in a lot of places. When we were first married your mother wanted to go to Spain or Argentina or somewhere, but this is a hell of a lot better.'

Perhaps that is why my mum cries when the southerly winds rip in over Moa Point and up over the Miramar North hills, trapping us miles from the nearest shop and library and anything else and doing it for day after cold, bleak day. She came from rural New South Wales. Her parents died when she was young, leaving her and her two brothers to work the farm. It couldn't support them. World War II came along and made the decision for them.

A phone call to the nuns at the Mater Hospital in North Sydney saw her travelling up from Moss Vale to become a student nurse. The wartime atmosphere broke the relentless, closely supervised work. The

Yanks were in town. Thousands of bright-eyed young GIs swarmed all over Sydney, wanting young nurses as dates, before going off to Tarawa, Guadalcanal, places no one had ever heard of and where many of them would die, returning in coffins.

A holiday to see some relatives on the West Coast of the South Island led her to Wellington, where she met my dad. It would be over twenty years before she left for Auckland. Three years later she made it to her Spain, or as close as New Zealand gets: a house overlooking Auckland's Hauraki Gulf.

That is ahead. Now she is in the house in Nevay Road chasing John, my next-youngest brother, outside to play and to take little Tony with him. Jane, our sister, is in the living room reading about Spanish castles, princesses and love.

It is quiet out on the harbour. The occasional 'flop' from the wet sack, and the water tinkling against the sides of the dinghy and nothing else. My father has gone quiet, almost sleepy.

After three hours of near-silence he comes to life, looks around and decides. 'We better be getting back in!'

He lifts the oars, fits them through the rowlocks and begins quietly, easily pulling the dinghy back towards the shore, and the little boatshed he rents in Karaka Bay. Rowing is easy for him. He is strong, with powerful forearms, the product of years of wrestling training during the long Depression days, fifteen years before.

'You navigate.'

'You are right on target.'

'Good on you. That's good.'

Two hundred yards later we are on land. The boat goes into the shed and we are in the Ford Popular, heading for home. 'You've had a good afternoon, haven't you?' Dad asks.

'Yes Dad.'

'This is better than the soccer, isn't it?'

'Yes Dad.'

It's too late for the soccer, so there is nothing to be done about that now. Disagreeing is a path to trouble. Get along by going along. 'Yup, fishing's better.'

My dad beams and rubs his hand on the top of my head. I look around at him and smile. Whoops. It might be a mistake to overdo this, in case the future is full of sitting in a little dinghy and no soccer. 'But I still like soccer a lot!' I remind him.

'Of course son, but fishing is good too, isn't it.'

This is heading towards Fishing versus Soccer, and a competition between What Dad Likes versus What I Like. I'll lose.

'They are both terrific.'

'That's my boy.'

He looks ahead. Everything might be all right.

When we get out of the Ford Popular, to carry the fishing gear and the sack of snapper up to the house, I stop for a moment when we reach the back door. The view from there is amazing. You can see from the city side of Petone and the Hutt Valley all the way down to the heads, all that gunmetal blue water, with the flashes of whitecaps starting to appear on it. The clouds are inky dark now. There's another gale on the way. I don't care. I'm home.

The sack of fish goes into the kitchen sink. My father finds a bottle of beer, opens it and pours himself a long glassful. He savours it, licking away the little circle of froth around his mouth. He stands in the kitchen, letting the soothing power of beer reach out right through his body. 'Terrific afternoon. There's four good snapper there.'

'Good,' Mum answers, flat and matter-of-fact.

'Were you all right? You sound a bit angry.'

'I've had all the kids all afternoon and I'm tired.'

'I took Denis.'

'Good. That's a start.'

He has decided he is not going to get anywhere. 'Pardon me! I'll get changed out of these clothes.'

His sarcasm misses the target. 'There are the baths to be run and they'll all want stories read,' she says.

'I'm going. I'm going.'

She looks at the sack in the sink. There is a movement. The fish are still alive. Meaning the fish have not been gutted. Someone is going to have to kill them, by driving a thin-bladed knife into the tops of their heads, then slit up the belly. A finger goes in and sweeps out the blue and red and stringy guts. This is done under cold running water to sweep the innards out into the Wellington stormwater system.

'You haven't gutted the fish!'

A distant 'No.'

This adds to her annoyance. She glances over at the oven. We won't be eating fish tonight. She has already bet against him bringing any fish home by going ahead and making a mince pie for dinner. It is in the oven starting to go nicely golden. The potatoes are baking alongside it. A pot of vegetables is bubbling away on the top of the stove. She looks around. The boys are getting manic. Blood sugar levels are getting low. There might be only one last burst of play left in them.

'Denis, John. Out! Go and play outside. Take Tony with you!'

John and I have seen that expression before, and heard her use that tone. We know surrender is best. But taking Tony? That's a problem. He is too little to be any good at soccer.

John had been gathered up by the neighbours and taken to the Basin Reserve. He saw Marist beat Miramar Rangers 4–3, a massive upset in Wellington soccer. He had been in a crowd of a hundred Miramar Rangers fans and Marist supporters; a small, disconsolate band of Wellington's lost and lonely Irishmen.

This win gives Marist vast prestige as we line up on the lawn and get ready to start our two-and-a-half player international soccer match. Prestige or not, John is not going to miss his chance.

'I am going to be the All Blacks,' he announces.

'What about Marist? They beat Miramar Rangers!' I want to be the All Blacks, but can't, because it is his turn to pick the teams.

'I'm the All Blacks,' he says again, just in case I missed the point.

'All right. I'll be the Springboks then! Let's kick off!'

'Waaaaaa.' This is Tony. He doesn't have an allocated name and he wants one. He is nearly three and if he is going to play he's going to be called something better than 'Tony'.

'You can be Marist.'

His howl of indignation stops instantly.

John and I both know the importance of Marist's win over Miramar Suburbs.

By Monday the dreadful news will have completed its loop around the Miramar Peninsula. The kids going to Miramar Central and Miramar North, the sources of Miramar Rangers' strength, will want to restore pride by taking a Catholic scalp, or at the very least a Catholic cap and tie, and be willing to die in the effort.

It is going to make it very tricky on Monday's Fortification Road bus. We are going to have to be very, very careful not to provoke trouble. At the same time we will make sure everyone knows Marist beat Miramar Rangers.

But that is Monday. This is Saturday. We have the All Blacks and the Springboks, with Marist swinging his little leg hoping to kick with the ball.

'Waaaaaaaa. I haven't had a kick yet.' Marist is not happy, and making sure everyone knows it.

It stops the Springbok surge on the All Blacks' goal. Both the All Blacks and Springboks suspect Marist knows exactly what he is doing, that if he runs howling and angry to an already frazzled mother she will become a Commission of Inquiry into the question of unfairness by the All Blacks and Springboks against Marist. The result would be pre-ordained. The commission would look around for the biggest participants and find them guilty.

The ball is placed in front of a now-smiling Marist.

Marist's little leg swings back, and flies through, connecting perfectly. The ball flies over the carrots and the beans to rest gently among the cabbages, in the opposite direction to the goal. Marist beams with joy. He also keeps quiet, his baby-teeth smile of pride shining over the land.

Mum watches through the kitchen window. All is well. Tony is smiling, so she won't get a tearful little boy demanding justice. He looks very tired, so he is going to have to be handled carefully if he is to be got through the bath, fed and into bed without a tantrum.

Jane is still reading her book. Mum looks at the picture of the sunny Spanish castle on the cover and tries not to look at the fierce, dark clouds dropping down over the Tararua Ranges over on the other side of the bleak-looking harbour. She looks at the pie, trying not to think about what might have been if she had got her way and touched down in Seville or Barcelona.

Dad is still in the bedroom. He is probably having a quick nap. It is all catching up on him: the beer with Jim Graham, the afternoon in the fresh air, and then another bottle of beer as soon as he walked in the door. His mother is also up in her room. With any luck she will be in a snit and want to eat on her own. There is always the chance they will have to teach her about knives and forks for the third time this week. Her brain has gone, and no one knows from one minute to the next what will happen, or what she will remember. There are times when it drives everyone a bit mad.

The old woman has only one consistent thought.

miramar DOG

This tall Australian woman has taken away her son.
The fact she rescued him from a beer-drenched, lonely
unhappiness, and got him through his accounting
exams, is not relevant information. She hates, surly and
silent and mercifully, mostly invisible.

The pie is ready. The potatoes look cooked and the
vegetables have only a few seconds of life before the
boiling water leaches out the last traces of iron and
minerals.

Marist is being told, 'You kicked the ball the wrong
way.'

He doesn't know which is the right way, so he falls
back on 'I did, I did too.'

Marist doesn't like the tone of voice being used
against him, but has decided it is not sufficiently bad
enough to require bringing in the Commission of
Inquiry. His moment has passed. The Commission of
Inquiry is busy with getting the dinner from kitchen to
dining room table.

chapter four

From the window of the public bar of the Shamrock Hotel in Thorndon the drinkers could see Parliament, whose laws forced bars to stop serving at six o'clock. The parliamentarians didn't have to worry about this. Their bar, Bellamy's, was open until late at night.

At the Shamrock the bells began ringing the ten to six warning. Time to fill the last round of jugs for the last session in the atmosphere of smoky, noisy, cheerfully rough maleness.

In a corner my Uncle Jack was asked, — What are ya doin' tonight, Jack?

— Probably go out and see me brother, out in Miramar.

— Bugger that. We're goin' round ta Sandy's.

Sandy's was a Tinakori Road slygrog, normally safe enough for an evening's drinking.

— Nah, you can go without me. Me brother has another baby, little boy named Tony.

— Jack, mate. He's a Mickey Doolan. He's always gonna be having another kid. C'mon up to Sandy's.

— Nah. I'll have another jug, then I'll go round ta the Green Parrot, get a feed, and then I'll get a taxi and head out there.

— You can go out there any night you like!

— You're broke, aren't ya. You're wanting me to go to Sandy's cause you haven't got any money to pay his prices. Jack was triumphant.

— I'm not broke!

— Then ya got nothin' ta worry about, have ya. More triumph.

— Fuck ya then.

Jack didn't bother getting another jug, even though Fred was looking up at the clock, and pointedly down at his empty jug. He walked out of the bar, and was lucky. A taxi was going past. He held up his hand. Even more luck. It stopped and he climbed before the driver to let him see if he was drunk or not.

— Round to the Green Parrot.

The driver sighed. He should have known better than to be out at this time of day. Nothing but bloody drunks. This was another one, hoping a steak, eggs and chips and a pile of buttered bread would mop up an afternoon in the pub. Better keep smiling, get him where he wants to go and hope he doesn't throw up in the cab.

chapter five

Father Bannon was in his little
office at the back of the priests' house, making lists.
There was nothing new about this. He was always
making lists. This one was of people he could ask to
help with rapid-raffle nights to raise money for the
church building fund. The names were mostly Irish,
Scots, English and Welsh, but a few names ending in
'ski' had begun appearing on his lists, the Polish
Catholics arriving from Europe's refugee camps. Not

many Italians, even though there were lots of them in Wellington. They had all taken one look at Miramar and headed for Island Bay; closer to the water, sheltered for their fishing boats and with a more Mediterranean atmosphere.

The Yugoslav people were also looking Wellington over, and heading for Auckland, especially west Auckland, as quickly as they could scrape up the price of a train ticket. Father Bannon could not understand this. Wasn't Miramar just the quietest, most peaceful place for young Catholic families to be bringing up their children under the kind but firm spiritual guidance provided by their priest?

Kevin Edwards' name was high on the list. But then, it always was. He would work all the hours in the world for the Church, and it helped if there was a sociable beer or two afterwards. His wonderful wife, Colleen, was there on the Ladies Committee, and hadn't she worked for days sewing the new vestments for the parish? Any priest anywhere would be proud to have such solid people behind him in his bringing the faith to the world.

Lord heavens. It was nearly eight o'clock. It was time to be thinking about bed. He was up for an early start, the 8am Mass up at Miramar North and then back for the next three Masses at the church in Miramar Avenue.

He would be finished about twelve. He could hop in his little car and take the run up to Nevay Road and have a lovely bit of lunch with the Edwards family. They did a beautiful roast lamb on Sundays, and there were all those fine children running around. It was a very pleasant atmosphere, especially if Kevin produced a bottle or two of Mission Vineyard wine. Then he frowned.

I suppose I'll have to take Father Reilly, he thought, but God knows he's going to have to make a few contacts of his own if he isn't going to be stuck here in the house and eating cold sausage all the time. He's a bit useless and he hasn't really found his bearings. Perhaps he should be back in Ireland. He'll go simple and mad if he doesn't find something to occupy himself. Pity he couldn't be more like the Edwards clan, the sort of solid dependable rocks Jesus himself chose for the founding of the Church.

chapter six

Mum is getting tired now, forcing herself to get everyone through the dinner. She is not having too many problems. The pie, potato and vegetables are disappearing into hungry little mouths without a hint of a complaint.

Dad commands a 'What do you say to your mother?' It's the cue for all of us to say, 'Thank you Mum.'

Dad adds his, 'That was terrific!' and looks around for dissenters. We all take the hint and nod a vigorous agreement.

The bath is full and hot. The first two, Tony and Jane, are marched off, to be thoroughly soaped, rinsed, dried, pyjama'd and led off to be read stories from their favourite books. Although the stories are short they need to be read several times with varying inflexions. On the third or fourth reading the listener is feeling completely secure and drops off to sleep. By then the next wave will have stepped on to the bath-and-soap conveyer belt, and be almost ready for their readings.

As Mum goes past their bedroom she catches a whiff of something smelling of fish and salt. If it is another sack of fish, homicide will not be out of the question. It comes from the clothes my dad had worn this afternoon. They are piled on the floor, where he has kicked them in the general direction of the wardrobe. She frowns and then realises this is a slight improvement on his early days. He had been an officer on board ship where he had stewards to clean up after him. They had taken over where his mother had left off in following him around and cleaning up after him.

Dad is coming back from reading Tony and Jane their stories. Both of them are asleep now. That leaves John and me. Once we are asleep they can pile the wood in the fireplace and sit in the semi-dark looking at the flames. By ten they will be in bed, exhausted. Sunday morning is an early start, getting everyone dressed and out for the eight o'clock Mass down at the Miramar North School hall.

John and I are in our beds, groggy with tiredness, dinner and the hot water, but still awake. There is always a remote chance of more excitement. Uncle Jack might turn up. We would know because there would be the slam of a taxi door and he would yell a 'thanks mate!' and stumble out on to the footpath. He would heft his grey cardboard carton, with its six quart bottles of Red Band, under his arm and begin his wobbly march on our back door. He would thump it until my Dad opened it. The light would go on and he would flop down on a dining room chair, and open the first of his bottles of beer.

We like Jack. He always makes a fuss of us, his big rough carpenter's hands mussing our hair, and sitting us at the table while he tells us stories about World War II. We knew them all by heart, but that doesn't matter, as long as we are part of the fun. Sometimes he gets my dad singing songs, *Maori Battalion*, *Danny Boy* or *Kevin Barry* mostly, and they usually forget the words, picking up speed when they reach the choruses.

Jack hasn't turned up, so I have started wondering about the fish. They are still in their sack. Mum had taken them out of the sink and put them in a bucket, so she and Dad could wash and dry the dinner dishes.

Just before dinner I heard him say, 'They should be gutted!'

She snapped back, 'Yes, they probably should be.'

He persisted. 'Four good snapper there. Get a couple of good dinners there.' He was hoping she would take the hint and gut them. He even tried a hopeful, 'Probably a bit too late to flick a couple of them in the oven?'

We saw her grip tighten on the big, sharp kitchen knife.

She laughed about it later, over a cup of tea with Mrs

Graham and Mrs Dayton. While no jury with women on it would convict, unfortunately there weren't too many juries with women on them. And who would look after the kids?

Besides, she might end up at Central with that cold-eyed Murray McCarthy sitting there probing away at everything in her entire existence, giving everything the worst possible meaning and trying to make her confess. That was enough to stop anyone even thinking about doing anything. She liked his wife but was always a little bit scared of something dark she sensed in him. She was never sure what it was, the violence, the hate or the rumours he hounded people, and planted evidence. But it was there.

All that only took a minute. They were quickly on to happier, more interesting things. She settled for, 'Yes Kev, it is too late to flick the fish in the oven.' Her tone convinced him not to make too much of it.

Now, at last, all the children are in bed. His mother has dropped off to sleep and won't be bothering anyone till the morning. She's had her 'medicine'. Every night she dosed herself with three large tablespoonsful of cheap, raw sherry. Drinking alcohol from the bottle, via a glass, is a sinful thing done by alcoholics and people to be shamed and avoided. Taking it from the tablespoon makes it 'medicine', so every night she happily drinks herself into oblivion, and calls it healing.

Mum and Dad's fire is an hour old. It is burning gently, the soft light flickering around the room. It is slowly dying, because they aren't putting any more coal on it. Mum's head is on Dad's shoulder. The radio plays.

The book reviews are over. Dinner music has ended. The request session is underway. Someone from Temuka wants something by John McCormack. The tenor's lachrymose voice fills our living room. Dad has Saturday night's *Evening Post* spread over his lap. His head drops down on his chest, and jerks up again as he tries to stay awake.

It is Mum who hears it first, even though it is a good two hundred yards away, down on the road. It is a car door closing.

'Oh God, no! Not tonight!'

She rubs her eyes and looks out the window. There he is, Jack, the powerfully built brother-in-law, with his grey carton of half a dozen bottles of beer standing beside the taxi.

'Oh God!'

Dad comes to life, grabbing at the *Evening Post* as it drops off his lap to the floor. 'What's the matter?'

'Jack's here!'

'Gosh. We haven't seen him for a while!'

'He's not to stay for hours. He has to go home.'

'He'll hear you.'

'I don't care. The kids are all asleep and I want them to stay that way.'

'All right. I'll do my best to get him to keep it down!'

They have to get to the door before Jack, he does not understand the concept of tapping on a door. If he knocks, he gets close to bashing it down in case the world does not want to answer him. The thought of this frightens Jack. He lives in a single room in Thorndon, and gets lonely. If he finds himself out here on the top of Miramar and there is no one home, it becomes a wasted trip, with only his room, or a slygrog, ahead of him. So he pounds on our back door.

He sighs. It is all right. There are footsteps from inside.

'Kev, how are you!' It is a beery bonhomie.

'C'mon in, Jack.'

He lifts his carton of beer bottles. 'There you are Kev. There's six live soldiers there, waiting to be turned into dead Marines!' He hands them over and smiles his broken-toothed grin.

Mum hears the first of the children waking up and shuts her eyes in frustration. This is the last thing she wants. She goes into the kitchen and holds her head in her hands, trying to cry with the tiredness and frustration of suddenly having a one-man party arrive, demanding time, attention and energy.

She looks around and sees the sack of snapper. She picks up the sack, looks in and pulls out a fish, dropping it on a wooden cutting board. She picks up a sharp knife. It is this or sitting out there and listening to the old stories of World War II and the Depression. She looks down at the fish's cold, dead eye.

'I know how you feel!'

She picks up the knife, holds the fish on the wooden board. She stabs it in the top of the head.

chapter seven

'Time for the beer!'

It nine o'clock on a wet and getting-windy
Wellington Friday night. It is rapid raffle night. John
and I wanted to go but weren't allowed. We had to wait
until later to find out what happened after the
fundraising committee for the Miramar Catholic
Church shoved through the door of the hall next to the
Newtown Catholic Church.

As they shrugged off the raindrops, the men could

not help but keep their eyes downcast for a moment, to avoid being intimidated by the rows of portraits of bleak-faced priests and bishops staring down from the walls. This never lasted long. A beer or two and they would be looking up, sideways or anywhere else they chose. After three or four beers the priests and bishops didn't exist.

They had walked up the hill from the butcher's shop down on Adelaide Road after two solid hours of selling rapid raffle tickets to the Newtown people, mostly the poor and pensioners, usually both.

Now it was time for more important things.

'Got that beer open yet?'

The rapid-raffle men were not the only ones busily setting up the trestle tables, turning them into a rough little bar. Some had had nothing to do with the rapid-raffles. They were here for the beer. Over the last two years the 'coupla beers' after the rapid-raffles had grown into a thriving, profitable and unlicensed bar.

It made almost as much money for the church fund as the raffles.

'There are people back here dyin' of thirst!'

Sid was always late, wheezing his way into the hall, loaded under three big wire trays of glasses. 'We oughta forget these friggin' raffles. Cuts inta the drinkin' time,' he grumbled.

No one took any notice of him. They would wait. They were not going anywhere else, because this was the perfect excuse to get out of the house. Some had had arguments with wives who didn't like seeing their husbands weaving out for the second skinful of beer for the day, after filling up before the bell rang for the pub's six o'clock close. The wives worried that they might crash their cars, get into fights or fall out a window, turning them from wives to widows. Miramar was not a good place to be a widow. They started married men thinking about life outside marriage, which made married women begin to think about life inside marriage. These could be unsettling thoughts. Who knew where they would end?

'Got that keg spiked yet?'

Sid had the mallet and the pouring tap for the big steel keg. There was a cheer as he lifted the mallet. He smashed it down and pushed in the pouring tap. As always, he did it without spilling a drop. Sid's skill with the mallet was admired far more than that of Rodin and the rest of the sculptors lying dead in the faded unread sets of the *Encyclopaedia Britannica* at home.

'Three cheers for Sid!'

'Bugger that. Three glasses for Sid!'

The laughter and cheering floated up to the roof. Glasses and wire trays clinked. Coins and notes dropped into the little chocolate tin Sid used as a till. 'Let the beer begin!'

By now everyone except my father and another accountant, one who worked at Accounts Payable for the Ministry of Works, was around the trestle-table bar.

They had a table of their own, where they solemnly counted the money.

'Don't forget about us.' That was my father, apt to become uncomfortable and twitchy when he was around beer and none of it was coming his way.

'No worries, mate. Always got a beer for the bean counters!'

My father glowered back. When it was 9pm at night he was Kev the rapid-raffle worker and Catholic father, not Kev the bean counter, a creature who inhabited his clothes from 8.30am on Monday morning until 4.30pm on Friday and feared by those wanting to spend government money.

The Ministry of Works man had pulled up a chair beside him. They were a matched pair, the accountants, my father and Donald. Both were strongly built ex-servicemen, and both had a worldly-wise look, with years of the great outdoors and smoky public bars behind them.

A frothing seven-oz glass of Red Band beer plonked down beside Dad's left hand. 'There you go, Kev. Don't spill it on the money!'

When the war ended, both had found themselves single and adrift in Wellington. Both flirted with the Communist Party, having decided that spending five years fighting fascism was enough reason to try and stop it turning up in Wellington. Both tired of the endless debates about the class struggle and both of them had drifted away.

'There you go mate. One for you too.'

That was a beer for Donald. He had stayed a year with the Commos before he too drifted away. Both were looking for something to do, which took them more or less by accident into the next adventure, marriage. They cashed in their government assistance credits for ex-servicemen and trooped off to Victoria University to study whatever they thought would get them a good living the quickest. This turned out to be accountancy. While they had had near-identical lives, they could not remember meeting each other until the rapid-raffle nights.

'Never mind the glasses, Sid. Just fill the jugs.'

'No jugs for youse jokers, not without paying for them first.'

'You sound like my missus.'

'If I was your missus you'd be paying first.'

'Talking like that must mean you *were* my missus.'

The laughter was getting louder. The beer smoothed away thought of bosses, wives and kids. Then there was the reassuring sight of the two accountants slaving away down at the end of the hall behind respectable-sized piles of coins. It looked as if there would be a profit. This improved the mood, grounds for calling for another round of beers.

The notes were counted, folded and dropped into the small canvas bag on the table in front of my father. The half-crowns and florins were in neat stacks. The shillings, sixpences and threepenny pieces were being marshalled into line. The pennies and halfpennies were still sprayed freely and carelessly out across one end of the table. This would not last. In the competition between their disorder and the two accountants, they would always lose.

Word around the bar was that the accountants were down to the pennies. It was now considered safe to give them another beer. 'Give 'em a thrill. Give 'em another glass. Better make it a pony, though. Don't want 'em to lose count!'

My father looked up. Huh! He might be an accountant, but he knew all about thrills and he definitely knew all about beer. The only good thing was the 'bean counter' crap seemed to have stopped.

'Bean counters never lose count.' That was Johnny, a grim man who did not like accountants. He lost his business after a tax audit and never bounced back, dwelling endlessly on the injustice. He would eventually have a heart attack, on the toilet while straining against constipation.

My father did not get a chance to shout anything back. There was a commotion at the door. People went quiet, remembering that no one had felt the need to wrestle with the paperwork needed for temporary liquor licences. This might be trouble.

chapter eight

It was all right. It was the next wave of men arriving from the butcher's shop. They had been making sure it was properly locked, and taken the spare prizes around to a friend's lock-up garage.

'What about a beer? Some of us walked up from the shop. That's five hundred yards. We got the dust of Newtown in our throats. Shocking thought.'

'Your missus sniffs beer on you that's all you'll be getting.'

'All the more reason! I need a night's sleep. You don't want to have to haul the old John Thomas out, dob it in 'er and think of England more than once a month. Ruins yer drinking!'

This was Blue, a little ex-submariner who worked on the Wellington City Council carpentry gangs. There was a little silence when he mentioned his sex life. Blue did not have one. When he'd had a chimney fire at his place and the firemen shoved him and Mary out on the footpath, it came out that they had separate bedrooms. But people liked Blue so they let him say what he liked. There was a worry or two over how much he drank, and he'd been known to belt Mary around when he was too lit up. On the other hand, he was always reliable for rapid raffles and work round the parish.

'There you go, Blue. Get that down yer.' The keg gave up another big glassful. The glass went through the pack to Blue. His threepence went back the other way. The beer went straight into Blue. Less than two minutes later another glass of beer and another of Blue's threepenny pieces crossed each other in the crowd.

'Cheers. Ah, that's a bloody good drop. But then any drop is bloody good.'

That was Arthur, general manager of the timber yard near Rongotai airport. Twenty blokes. Big job. Lot of responsibility. No one could blame a man for having a beer after work after a hard day, or a week or a month of that. Arthur was another who never missed a Friday night of selling raffle tickets to Newtown pensioners and the fathers of big families. The man was a saint.

'Mavis'll be on her knees about now.' Mavis was Arthur's wife.

Arthur didn't say anything, just smiled his big smile and drained his glass.

'Hey Arthur, does she wait till you get home or have you got a bloody long one? It'd have to be a couple miles long.' Rowdy laughter. 'How'd yer keep it in yer shorts when you were packing in the scrum up at the Park.'

'No, no, no. Those days are over.' Arthur was chuckling. 'She'll be on her knees in prayer, mate. She'll be praying I get nicked for driving under the influence!'

Another quick little moment of silence. How many other wives were praying for the same thing, that their husbands would end up at Taranaki Street police station, being fingerprinted and photographed on the way to court and to losing their licences? Of course they would get the licences back for work, but not for the weekends. That meant no footy, no rapid raffles, no anything. They'd be left with long weekends of working around the house. None wanted to contemplate that thought. It was too depressing.

'Here's the only influence you need. Have another one!'

'That's the right sort of influence for me.'

'You blokes better stand aside, in case Arthur wants to come through. He's got a thing in there that can reach Miramar. He oughta be one of those knights on a horse jousting with the enemy.'

The laughter cut through what had become a thick cloud of cigarette smoke.

There was a sound at the door. Heads turned, but

again it was all right. The Newtown church fundraising committee had arrived.

'Another twenty throats fresh from the road.'

'Bloody oath, and we aren't here to mess around. Somebody get pouring.'

Their rapid-raffle night was in distant Thorndon, forced there in the search for a butcher's shop, the perfect venue for rapid-raffle nights. There was never anything breakable in them and all the stock was safely in the chiller, so there were never any problems with thieves.

A Miramar man owned the best-located butcher shop in Adelaide Road. As soon as his concerns about his son not getting a place in the Marist Rugby Club fifth-grade team had been cleared up, his shop was open to the Miramar fundraisers. This left the Newtown Catholic fundraisers disgruntled and having to roam Wellington looking for a butcher shop of their own. They were turned away in Petone, Kilbirnie, Khandallah, Seatoun, Karori, Wadestown, Island Bay and Oriental Bay. Finally they found a shop in Thorndon, but only after a long, delicate negotiation and much appealing to the butcher's softer, kindly side.

Finally, after convincing him of the great contribution he would make to his beloved Church and how his soul would live in heaven, he gave way. Yes, the men from Newtown could use his shop, and because it was for the faith he would reduce his cut from five per cent down to 2.5 of the takings. 'Oh, and me brother-in-law's gotta be there too. He's an accountant, and he'll be coming along to make sure me cut comes out.' Bared teeth masqueraded as smiles when they shook hands on the deal.

The Newtown team's cash counters — the church man and the butcher's brother-in-law — pulled up chairs beside my father and Donald from the Ministry of Works. They would not take their eyes off each other.

One was determined the 2.5 per cent deduction would not drift up to four or five per cent. The other was keen to keep the 2.5 per cent at around one per cent. These financial problems always occurred when one or the other made the mistake of slipping away to the toilet.

The butcher's brother-in-law piped up. 'Any chance of a couple of beers down this end of the place?'

Someone gave him a full jug and two glasses. No one asked him to pay. It was futile. Last week he dipped into the takings to pay for his beer and refused to deduct it from the 2.5 per cent. They gave him the beer in the hope that he might be forced to the toilet — the takings total would be quickly adjusted downwards while he was gone.

The Newtown rapid-raffle night's half crowns, florins, shillings, sixpences, threepenny bits and pennies slid out over the table. My father and Ministry of Works drained their glasses, trying to decide whether they wanted to get involved with helping these two, or make a start on some serious drinking.

'Hide the beer! Here's Murray and Ted!'

Murray McCarthy was here, with Ted Andrew in tow. The two policemen were obviously off-duty, so they would not be getting awkward about all the beer being sold illegally.

'There you are Ted. Get that down you.'

'Good on you, mate.'

'There you go, Murray.'

It never occurred to anyone to even think of asking Murray or Ted to pay for their beer. They were police. In Wellington, and after hours, they always drank free. The row of backs and shoulders around the trestle table eased to create a little corridor for them.

'What about another one, Murray?'

'Only just got this one. Yer not trying to get me smashed are yer.' Murray was sharp, aggressive.

'Gawd no, Murray. No, no. Not at all.'

'That's all right then.'

The cigarette smoke was making it hard to see from one side of the hall to the other. The smell of beer was over everything. At least one glassful had been spilt on the floor. Other drinkers were letting smaller amounts slop out of their glasses. The beer mixed with the cigarette ash, the stubbed-out butts and the mud and dogshit carried in on the soles of the shoes. Not that they had to worry. The Ladies Committee would be in to clean it up first thing next morning, getting it tidy before the ballet kids arrived.

Ted had found himself in the centre of the crowd, accepting the free beers as they came along, grinning his uneven-toothed smile as each glass disappeared into his huge paw. Ted was a solid 'kick 'em in the bum' policeman; big, rough and always taking the straightest line to solving any problem. When he was out on the beat, Ted always liked to be in control of a situation. If he felt this was not so, there was hell and terror and broken bones until others saw his point of view. He was also the only one who dared howl out, 'Hey Muzza. Aren't ya drinkin?'

Murray smiled back and lifted his glass, so everyone would see he was one of the blokes and having a beer. But not too much. Murray McCarthy always preferred to be on the sidelines, watching. While Ted walked the beat and kicked bums, Murray swam in deeper waters.

'Yeah, I'm drinkin.' It was a surly mutter.

But then Murray was almost always surly. He was always cursing marrying a Catholic. She had a kid every year, and she forced him to come out and help with rapid-raffle nights. The only good thing about it was he got a beer afterwards. The trouble was he was drinking with civilians. He always preferred drinking with other police. They were his people and they understood each other. The only time anyone had seen him genuinely happy was when he caught homosexuals in the act and could arrest them, preferrably violently.

My father was pushing up to the front.

'Here you go, Kev.' Another beer for my father.

'We've made £9 15s 6d!'

Anything over £8 was good. 'Good on yer' and 'Bloody good effort' spun around the hall, becoming grounds for another beer for everyone.

The Newtown group's accountant took my father's place. '£4 8s.' Another cheer. That was a good effort for them, because everyone knew Thorndon was a much tougher place to sell raffle tickets. Too many boarding houses and criminals, and there was Parliament just over the road. It all added up to a shifting population, which everyone knew was no good for rapid raffles. Who wanted a meat pack when the next week they might be in Palmerston North, Australia, or Mount Crawford prison?

There was no more time for mulling over these things. Suddenly there were other, more pressing matters to be thinking about.

chapter nine

The ever-watchful Murray saw them coming first, glimpsing the tops of the policemen's helmets as they tip-toed into position, ready to begin the raid on the hall.

'Shit! Ted! Come on.'

Ted might not have been too bright, but he understood exactly what was happening. The new senior sergeant at Wellington Central was out to enforce the liquor laws. Protestant bastard.

Both Murray and Ted were across the hall in three strides. They had the window open and they were gone, out into the night. There was a scuffle.

'Got you, ya Tyke prick.'

'No you bloody haven't.'

There was the thump of a punch to the stomach and air seeping out of a suddenly-dazed policeman. Once again Ted had taken the direct line to solving another problem. My father looked around. The police were at the door and would be inside in seconds. He sprinted down to the end of the hall, opened the lid on top of the piano and dropped the bag of money inside. There was a twang as the bag hit the low-register notes.

He did not hear this. He was halfway out the window. The policeman was standing bent over, holding his stomach and trying to regain his breathing. He stiffly straightened when he saw my father. 'I got ya. You bloody left-footer. You're arrested, ya bastard.'

My father charged, dropping his shoulder, hitting the policeman in the sternum, snapping his head back. His helmet flew off. He looked less than twenty years old. Too bad. My father swung his fist and hit him in the solar plexus. A stream of bad breath softly floated out from the policeman's mouth. My father was free. He glanced back. Arthur was being hauled back through the same window.

Inside the hall there was noise and yelling, with the police beginning to herd the 'criminal bloody Tykes', as the senior sergeant kept calling them, towards the side of the hall. He counted his catch. Eighteen of them, and the beer and the glasses and the wire trays and everything. They wouldn't be seeing any of that again. That was seized evidence, and if they had rented any of it then it was just too bad. He'd done his bit. He would tell his friends at the Poneke Rugby Club he'd kept the country safe for the breweries, and he'd lumbered a whole raft of Catholics. Who could ask for more?

'Youse blokes just keep still. You're all under arrest for breaching the liquor laws with after-hours trading and you're all goin' down to Central to get ya photos and yer fingerprints taken. If ya give any trouble you get trouble. Real trouble.'

That was his standard speech, one he had delivered hundreds of times in his twenty-five years in the police, usually to an audience of one, but sometimes to large groups, like this one.

Meanwhile Dad was hopping his way over a neighbour's fence, almost dodging a large dog which ripped a little bit of his right trouser leg, ruining a good suit.

The senior sergeant was looking out into the night. His constables were backing up the Black Marias. They had three of them, taking four people each. He did a quick head count. There were eighteen tykes. He was not going to get more vehicles. He had no chance — there were two other raids on tonight, one in Thorndon and the other in Seatoun, so all the vehicles were out. He'd just have to pack them in a bit tighter.

'I want ya to file out nice and tidy. Ya can forget about getting away. We can handle types like you. Criminals!' He spat the last word out with as much malice as he could manage, equating Catholics with the worst sex deviants ever caught committing mass murder.

Blue was glaring back. 'I get a chance at that bastard he'll lose the lot, baton and prick.'

'You can shut up. I'm not losin' anything, not to a little nutsack like you. I oughta charge ya with threatenin'. Could get ya inta Mount Crawford for a spell.'

'Bloody prick!'

'Come on Blue. Just shut up!'

'That's a good idea. You wanna listen to yer mates. Speaking good sense — for Catholic criminal bastards.'

'Bloody prick.'

'Get the Marias back up by the door. We're gonna have to double up a bit. Nothin' I can do about that, and that's as close to an apology as you're gonna get.'

My father had circled around and was on the other side of the road and up the hill. He was thanking the Lord that Newtown was a Labour electorate in a city run by a National-inclined council. It did not waste money on extra street lighting in Newtown, letting him edge up close enough to see what was happening.

The senior sergeant was strutting along the line of Catholics, until he found the one with the hall key. He took it. He ordered his constables to start removing the beer equipment and to lock up when he left. My father was close enough to hear voices from one of the Black Marias. Arthur was begging Sid, 'For God's sake, don't even think about farting till we get to Central.'

It was all over in a quarter of an hour. The police vans had gone, as had all the beer and the glasses. My father looked around the hall. The door was locked. So were the windows. The police had done a thorough job of securing the place. Unless he broke in, the rapid-raffle money was staying there till the morning.

He was not breaking in. He had had enough of police and crime for one night. He had other things to be doing. It was time for someone closer to God to get involved.

chapter ten

Twenty minutes later he was knocking on the door of the Miramar Presbytery.

The voice from inside was irritable. Father Bannon had gone to bed early. 'Who is it?'

'Kevin Edwards.'

The door opened. 'Kevin. It's after half-past ten. Good Lord, it's nearly eleven. What's the matter!'

'There's been a raid. They've all been done.'

Father Bannon stood aside to let my father in the

house, then disappeared into another room, swapping his pyjamas for a pair of trousers and a jersey. His twisted toenails were a dullish yellow colour.

'Sit down, Kev. Sit down.'

My father poured the story out, ending with, 'Is there anything you can do?'

Father Bannon shook his head. 'Oh no. It's a matter for the police and the courts.'

'All the fundraising committee were in there.'

'All of them?' Father Bannon frowned. This was serious. He had come from Upper Hutt, where a similar horror had befallen the Church, and the wives, good women every one of them, used it as an excuse to keep their husbands away from any Church event, bar Mass and Benediction. The parishioners had been generous when the plate went around at Mass, but they could not come close to matching the rapid-raffle take.

'You know, Kevin, it's not really a Church matter.' He was much less convincing.

'All the committee, Father, all of them.'

'Oh.' There was a long pause while Father Bannon digested this. 'Now Kevin, that's a terrible thing. We can't have good Catholic men sitting in there, when they should be home with their wives and their little ones.'

'Yes, Father.'

'Apart from yourself, did anyone else escape?'

'Murray and Ted.'

'Well, that's good for them of course. It's a pity, though. If there was a couple of their own caught, the police might not be so keen to make a fuss over the whole business.'

'I only hope we can get some of the men out for more fundraising. But, I think they've got everyone.' It was my father's only card and he was playing it over and over again. Finally, it worked.

Father Bannon lifted himself off his chair. 'Excuse me for a second, Kev. I'll give a call and see if there is any advice I can get from the higher authority.' He glanced up to indicate God, but he meant the Bishop.

My father later described this as the moment when he saw the Church's slow, ponderous but powerful engine clank into action, to begin crushing everything in its way.

'You wait here, Kev.'

He did, sitting on the couch straining to hear what was happening in the hallway. He heard Father Bannon dialling a number. Then, 'I know it's late. No, he hasn't got drunk and done anything. He's asleep. I just saw him an hour ago.'

'Drunk and done anything.' This was interesting. My father had thought the curate was a mild little chap who would never say 'boo' to any living thing. Obviously there was more to Father Reilly than he'd realised.

'The fund-raising committee. All of them! That's about £9 a week from the raffles and another 15 from the social hour afterward. That's £24 a week.' Father Bannon's voice rose. He was getting angry. 'That's £8 a week going straight into your diocese funds.'

That stopped my father thinking about the blokes

in jail. The accountant in him rose like an angry bull. Eight pounds a week, for nearly three years! That was hundreds of hard-earned pounds! No wonder the bishop and all the rest of them had so much money to do good work. And, no wonder the bloody building fund was struggling along. It was being milked for the diocese.

He did not trust himself to say anything to the priest. He knew what would happen. Father Bannon would dive behind his cassock and the dog collar and play the same cards, one after the other and always in the same order. There would be the speech about doing God's work, helping the less fortunate and how Mother Church helped where it was needed most. By the time he reached the part about a moral duty to help the less fortunate the battle would be over. No, better not start that, not tonight.

The priest came back.

'Are they going to help?'

'It's all in God's hands now.'

'Bloody hell.'

'Kevin, where are you going?'

Home, to explain where he had been, and then sleep. He would also be setting the alarm, to be back at the Newtown church hall at nine in the morning when the ballet girls arrived, to get the rapid-raffle money back.

In Karori James O'Hara was stumbling along the hall, blearily snapping on the light. The phone was ringing. He did not get telephone calls in the middle of the night, not anymore. He was a

Queen's Counsel, at the height of his profession. He was respected and respectable. These days his clients came from solicitors' referrals, not from the cellblock at Wellington Central.

— Yes! he snapped into the receiver. Then he changed his tone.

— Of course sir. Wellington Central. I'll certainly do what I can. Better not wait till morning. It might confuse the picture. Momentum builds up and it can be a wee bit difficult to turn the flow of it around.

He was already half-dressed. The Catholic Church might occasionally cry the poor mouth. But, by God, it paid its bills.

— What's going on dear? asked a sleepy voice from the bedroom.

— I've just had a call.

— You promised you weren't going to do those night calls any more. Isn't that why they made you a Queen's Counsel?

— It's all right. It's for a friend.

— Who?

— The Catholic Church.

— Them again! I wouldn't call them friends.

It was midnight when O'Hara walked into Wellington Central. The usually quiet police station looked like a busy railway station. Queues of people had been lined up in the cellblock, waiting to be processed. Policemen were standing around writing in notebooks and being busy.

The senior sergeant strode over when he saw O'Hara. — Nothing for you here. We got the tykes, the lot of 'em. Got 'em cold, selling beer up in Newtown. It's goin' ta court. They're getting convictions, the bloody pack of 'em. Criminals!

He managed to combine this with a sneer against Catholicism and a smug triumph at his good work. O'Hara stood for a second, fascinated at his ability to convey so much with so little.

— Can I have a list of the names.

— They clients of yours?

O'Hara and the senior sergeant had done this mating dance before. O'Hara would get his list, handed over as grudgingly as possible and he would have to wait as long as the senior sergeant could keep him. But, he would oblige O'Hara. O'Hara was important and complaints from him would be taken seriously.

— Yes.

— It's not typed yet. You might have to wait a while. Be about an hour. You can wait there. He waved O'Hara to the waiting room, the ochre walls covered with crime prevention posters and a brown linoleum floor saturated by decades of blood, beer and vomit.

O'Hara walked out into the street, to the pay phone on Lambton Quay. The voice answered, 'Central Police.'

— This is Colin Manning. I want to speak with the duty inspector. Colin Manning was a deputy commissioner of police.

Within seconds it was.

— Duty inspector here, sir!

— It's Jim O'Hara.

— Fuck Jim, I thought it was Manning. You impersonated a member of the police. That's a crime.

— I wouldn't have got past that pompous prick of a senior sergeant otherwise.

— You're out at that bloody pay phone, aren't you? Come round to the back door.

Inspector Mick Mahon opened the door for O'Hara. They walked upstairs, leaving the lights in the stairwell off. There was no point in letting everyone in the station know there were visitors. Mahon opened the door to the district commander's office, crossed to the liquor cabinet and pulled out a bottle of whisky. He poured two glasses, and handed one to O'Hara.

— You here for the Newtown ones, the Thorndon ones or the Seatoun one?

— One?

— Yeah, the cop out there, Arthur Foley, got a whisper from the duty sergeant. He got round and tipped them off before Super Senior Sergeant down there turned up. There was only the caretaker cleaning up. So he got lifted. Poor bugger's deaf. He can't figure out what happened. He made a guess about what they wanted, and wrote out a confession about having a garage full of hot radios. CIB's running round like they solved the mystery of the Marie Celeste.

— I'm here for the Newtown ones.

— Ted Andrew and Murray McCarthy were there, but they got away. Bopped a young cop on the way out. He's filed a complaint. Thinks I'm going to take notice of it, and that I'll be getting them up on charges. Dumb little prick's pissing in the wind. Murray'll put the copper's whole family in the Homo Register. That'll bugger them up. Mahon chortled at his joke.

— How many clients do I have, Mick?

— Eighteen of them. It is not going to be easy to lose that many in the paperwork, Jim. I found out the Senior Sergeant down there's deep in the Freemasons. There's dozens of them in the force, they hate us Catholics and they stick together like diarrhoea to old undies.

O'Hara shuddered at the thought of the Senior Sergeant's underpants. He decided to drain his glass quickly, hoping the whisky would turn his thoughts to anything else.

— I can spring 'em all on bail. No worries there. I'll get 'em out till Monday. If they go up tomorrow they'll get the JPs. There's another coupla bloody Masons who'll send 'em all up to Mount Crawford for the rest of the weekend.

O'Hara looked suitably shocked, but said nothing. He knew from experience the best thing to do was nothing. Mahon would sort it out. He always did.

— They go up Monday and they get Fred Scanlon on the bench. He remands 'em for a fortnight for pleas. I get Fred to have a word with Manning when they play golf on Wednesday. Fred bitches all the way round the back nine about clogging up the courts with half-baked liquor offences, how he's going to have to speak out from the bench about how the police are filling up the courts with this sorta garbage when there's real crime.

— Real crime?

— Someone kicked the side of Fred's car in.

O'Hara nodded his encouragement.

— I can get Jack Riddiford to send one of his little brats round from the *Dominion*, make sure they soak

up everything Fred says and stick it all over the paper—
that's if Manning doesn't come to the party. That'll piss
Manning off, 'cause he's up for Commissioner and
he doesn't want any fuck-ups or that prick from
Dunedin'll slip right past him. I reckon it all should be
enough to get this lot of charges flushed down the
crapper.

O'Hara sat still. He was going to get a fat fee,
guaranteed, from the Catholic diocese for getting the
Newtown men freed. If this kept going the way
Mahon was talking, there might not be anything left
for him to do. He decided to reduce the fee.
Fortunately the whisky nerve held through that little
crisis of conscience.

Mahon was looking thoughtfully at the whisky
bottle. He decided against having another shot. He
waved O'Hara to stay where he was and waddled out
to the nearest toilet, the women's. He turned on the light
and held up the bottle to the mirror until he could see
the small mark on the label. He carefully poured
enough water in to restore the level. He lumbered back
into the office, screwed the top back on the bottle and
put it in its place the cabinet.

—I'd offer you another one, Jim. Trouble is, with all
these arrests for liquor offences everyone is going to be
a bit touchy on the subject. Better not have too much of
it on me breath. Its a bit complicated, with them pulling
Frank Wilkins out of the drink.

—Complicated? O'Hara understood the word
'complicated'. Lawyers always did.

Mahon opened the door.

— Wouldn't be at all surprised if you don't end up a bit busier.

— A lot busier?

Mahon looked at him. His smile only lasted a second.

— There's things happening. There's a young girl run away from home up on Mount Victoria. It doesn't look good. Her father's been in here for a chat. He's had the phone books. Never said anything. Frank Wilkins' car has turned up in Marjoribanks Street. There's a lot stirring, Jimmy. If it really livens up it might be an idea to keep your appointment book clear.

O'Hara nodded. He hadn't done a murder case for a couple of years. He missed the excitement. He was always ready to get the wig and gown out.

— I can't see anyone getting in the dock for Frank, not yet. But you never know. They found a shambles up in Newtown. Blood, hair, all that shit.

If Mahon didn't think anyone would be getting into the dock he'd bet his house on exactly that; that no one would be troubling a judge. Still, there was always a chance. And it was possible someone might come to him for help because they were suspected, and wanted someone to deflect and muddy things. O'Hara could help there too.

Mahon opened the door to let him out.

— No one knows you were here. You go round the front and scream your head off about getting them out on bail. Let him give you a bit of abuse, but don't worry about it. If I turn up, you don't know me. I might have to have a bit of a flick at you too.

O'Hara was smiling a purring reassurance. Not a problem. Rules of the game.

Mahon opened the door to the street.

— We've gotta stick together, cause the Masons have got the whole place completely under control. We've got our backs right against the wall, mate.

As he trotted around to the front door, O'Hara struggled to think of anyone less against the wall than Inspector Mahon. He walked in the main entrance and began arguing for the charges to be dropped and his clients to be released. The senior sergeant was all but laughing in his face.

— Them criminals is going to get bail when I decide, and not before and they'll be going up in front of the courts and they'll get what's due to 'em.

O'Hara shrugged. — There's not much I can do.

— Nothing.

— I guess I'll be seeing you in court.

— Yeah. Are you finished? I got proper work to do, instead of hanging around chattin' with you.

Mahon swept past O'Hara. He snarled at the senior sergeant. — You been saying anything to that lawyer which could balls up our chances of getting a conviction.

— Um, no sir.

— I bloody hope not. If he gets them off, and there's no convictions at the end of this, I'm gonna have yer balls for me kids' marbles competition.

— Yes sir.

— Bail 'em till Monday.

— What about the JPs?

— Never mind the JPs. Bail 'em till Monday.

— But Scanlon is on the bench on Monday. He'll let 'em all go.

— That's none of our business. We don't decide the course of justice. Judges do that. Bail 'em till Monday.

— Yes sir.

— And don't look at me like that. That's insubordination. You'll be up on a charge if you don't perk yourself up.

— Yes sir.

— Give this lawyer his list, now.

The senior sergeant returned with the list. Mahon snatched it off him and thrust it at O'Hara. — There's your clients. None of them are getting questioned and they are all getting bail. You aren't getting any police facilities to interview them, so you might as well bugger off.

The senior sergeant looked pleased to see someone else on the end of Mahon's fire. O'Hara shrugged, took the list, and walked away to his car. Another night of fighting for justice was over and it was time to go home. There was only one thing left on the night's to-do list, figure out a way to wake his wife up without startling her so much that she didn't start wanting sex.

chapter eleven

At eight the next morning Dad was bouncing around, looking at his watch, wanting to get on his way to Newtown to get the rapid-raffle money back.

'If you go, you can take Denis and John with you.' My mum said. She was definite.

'It's just over to Newtown and back. It'll only be an hour.'

'Take Denis and John with you.'

No Denis and John meant no going to Newtown. He waved us in the direction of the road. We sprinted down the path to stand next to the car, in case there was a mistake and we were left behind.

Dad parked our Ford Popular outside the Newtown church hall.

'Damn!'

The door was open. The ballet girls were early. Mothers were around the door shooing their tutu'd youngsters inside.

My father walked in, aiming straight at the piano. A tired-looking woman of about sixty was sitting at the keyboard, a cigarette glued to her bottom lip. Cigarette or not, she managed to curl it when she glared at him.

'You bringing in the boys for ballet classes?'

My father stopped. 'No. I've come to collect something we left here last night.'

'Oh yeah, and what would that be? Place got raided last night. Tykes been runnin' a slygrog. Whole place stinks of beer.'

Her top lip curled back. Contempt seeped from each of her pores.

'I want to have a look in the piano.'

'There's nothing there.'

She realised that was a mistake, admitting she knew there had been something in the piano.

'There was when you came in this morning.'

'I said there's nothin' there now.'

There was a pause. The piano player and my father locked eyes, just like gunfighters in a western movie.

The quickest-drawing negotiator would end up with the money.

'There was money in there last night.'

'It's criminal money!'

'If it's criminal money then it should go to the police.'

The woman's eyes flickered.

Dad pushed on. 'I know exactly how much is in the bag, and I've got witnesses. The police will be wanting all of it, or they'll be wanting to charge someone with theft.'

The woman folded her arms across her chest. 'It's bloody hard, working here every Saturday mornin', playin' the piano for the daughters of rich kids.'

In the distance a twenty-five-year-old was lining up her little flock of ten-year-olds. 'Are you ready, Mrs Cudby? The *Nutcracker*, from the allegro in Act Two.'

Mrs Cudby let her head turn to the ballet teacher. 'I'm a bit busy for a coupla minutes. What about giving them another stretch?'

'The girls have done their stretches.'

'What about givin' them some more? Ya can't do too much stretching.'

'I don't think it's a good idea for the girls to be sitting down doing floor stretches in all this beer.'

Mrs Cudby muttered, 'They're gonna be spending the rest of their lives with beer and men. Might as well get used to it.'

'Sorry, Mrs Cudby, I didn't hear you.'

Mrs Cudby turned back to my father. 'You can get on yer way.'

'I want the money from the piano.'

'The criminal money.'

'It's rapid-raffle money, not beer money.'

'Corrupting bloody gambling money. Same thing.'

'Mrs Cudby, can we start? The girls are ready to start dancing.'

The woman muttered, 'Dunno why. None of 'em are any good. Most of 'em have got two left feet. They won't be able to dance their way out of a bad marriage any time in the next forty years.'

'I heard that, Mrs Cudby!'

'How much finder's fee?'

'Nothing. It's Church money.'

'Well then, you can get on yer way. I gotta play the piano.'

'The money!'

'How much?'

'Five bob.'

'Two pound.'

'Ten bob.'

'Mrs Cudby, could you please start playing the piano. The allegro in Act Two.'

'Bloody allegro in Act Two. Dunno why I ever learned to play the thing. Doin' this every Saturday! It's a life sentence for an old woman. One pound ten.'

'Seven and sixpence.'

'Mrs Cudby!'

'All right. What about a pound?'

'Done.'

Her bony hand reached into a vast cloth bag at her feet, flicked her knitting out of the way and fished out the grey canvas bag. She reached in, took out a pound note, held it up, so my father could see it. He nodded. She handed over the bag.

'Mrs Cudby!'

'Yeah, all right. Here we go.' Her hands rose over the keys and crashed down.

'The *Nutcracker*, not *Swan Lake*.'

'Sorry.' She shuffled the music again. Up went the hands, and again they crashed down. As my father turned us round to go back to the car, Mrs Cudby gave a big wink. Dad winked back. She smiled and bent to her piano playing. She had put her cigarette up on the top of the piano.

When my father got home he emptied the money out. He was proud of getting it all back, bar one pound. He was smugly telling us he was a good negotiator, and that he hoped we'd paid attention.

Then he went quiet. He was two pounds short. She'd already helped herself to a one pound note. Plus she negotiated another one from him. No wonder she gave in quickly. Dad was silent for a while after that. It was not till we had got through Kilbirnie that he smiled all the way home. He had a sense of humour and he knew when he was beaten, and this time he had been completely cleaned out.

chapter twelve

Other people have noticed that Marist beat Miramar Rangers. They also noted, something we missed, that this was more than an ordinary game. It was a Catham Cup elimination game. The 4-3 loss was the end of Miramar Rangers' hopes of getting their hands on a trophy.

Terry Taylor and James Wilson are Miramar North School kids and they are waiting at the bus stop for me and John to turn up. Two of them and two of us. That means there will be even odds if there is a fight. So there probably won't be one, because any eight-year-old knows you never start a fight unless you are sure you are going to win. You have to have the numbers stacked at least two-to-one on your side.

Although there isn't going to be a fight, that doesn't mean the rituals won't be observed. They live furthest from the bus stop, which makes them the visiting team, so they go first.

'Catholic dogs eat frogs!'

'Proddy pigs!'

'Catholic, Catholic. Pope Tyke. Pope Tyke!'

'Proddy pig. Proddy pig. Proddy pig!'

These are the opening lines of a ritual. The next stage is for honour to be appeased by a certain amount of pushing and shoving, including a grabbing and hurling away of school caps.

Today is different. There is a form of divine intervention at the bus stop. It is a man standing there, waiting for his bus. He is carrying a small toolbox, and none-too-happily looking forward to a long day of brutally hard labour in a quarry. He scowls, and grunts. We stop pushing and wait to see which religious group he is going to support. I am quietly confident about this, because if he looks like a labourer he is probably Catholic.

'Shuddup the bloody lota ya little prick bastards,' he growls. 'Knock it off, ya little shits.'

There is good news in this. There is no sign of religious hatred. He hates us all, without caring who is

Catholic and who is not. He keeps glaring at us, to make sure there is no more yelling.

Terry Taylor and James Wilson stand and wait until the bus arrives and we get on. When we do they start yelling at us again, safe from the quarry man's grumpiness.

Terry Taylor looks up. 'We'll get ya when we play ya next month. We'll kick ya heads in, and you'll get thrashed 10-0!'

John yells back, 'No ya won't. You're not good enough. You'll never be good enough!'

'You'll see! Catholic dogs!'

'Proddy pigs!'

'I told you bloody kids to shut up!'

He looks angry so we shut up, settling for exchanging the fingers sign with them.

There is nothing particularly personal in this. We know they have to go on like this because they know they are on the outside, having to cope with living near people—which is us—who are members of the One True Church, and who play in a better soccer team.

We are going to have to be a bit careful about this. Sooner or later we are going to have to end up playing against them, either for the school teams or in street games.

Our mothers make us play street soccer with them. We don't specially want to play with them, and we have found out that the fathers are on the side of their sons. James Wilson's dad is particularly tough, going on about not wanting his kid getting stuck with a 'crew of left-footers'. He's worried that if his eight-year-old son plays cricket and soccer up on the corner of Nevay and Fortification Roads he will end up under the 'evil influence of the friggin' Pope!'.

Mum is never sure whether he is joking about this. She heard about it when she had cups of tea and scones with some of the other mothers. They got the fresh-baked ones, with dates and sultanas in them. This is better food than she feeds her own flesh and blood — I asked for one of the date ones and got tossed a half-stale cheese job. It looked to me like a classic case of religious discrimination. When I tried to appeal this injustice I got chased out to play. On the way out I heard the mothers laughing about the father who didn't want his kid playing with Catholics. James' mother was saying that her boy playing with us 'means he isn't an only child. It makes him the middle one of five, your four and him.' That meant we would be stuck with him next time we had a street cricket game. Why couldn't his mother listen to his father?

The trouble is we have to admit we need him. He is also a good off-spin bowler and he slows his bowling down so Jane and Tony can get a hit.

Terry Taylor tends not to be as interested in playing. He likes to sit and read books and learn how to play chess and stuff. But when he is chased out to play with us he is an even better batter and bowler, and a good soccer player. We never tell him this, because he'll get a swelled head, and he might want to play all the time, and no one else will get a chance to win anything.

When John and I get to school Brother Brian, the headmaster, is standing there.

We are a bit scared of him. He's really big and when he yells he can be heard in every corner of the playground.

'Did you two get yelled at this morning?'

'Yes Brother Brian,' we say together.

'Was it because you are Catholics?'

We both nod.

'Did anyone hit you?'

'No, Brother Brian.'

The labourer must have told him. He was the only other one there. Before I can ask about this, Brother Brian is gone, walking away to where two of the Seatoun boys are arriving. When they say 'Yes' he turns and walks off towards Holy Cross School, where we used to go when we were just starting school and where they still teach the girls. Our sister Jane is over there somewhere in among the nuns and the other girls. We used to be allowed there, when we went to school, but not now. We are at the boys' school, and that means we are big, so we don't have anything to do with girls and dolls and cooking and stuff like that.

It takes a few days to find out what is going on.

Brother Brian lines us all up outside the classrooms. 'There have been some incidents, the sort of thing which we hoped had been put behind us forever in this country. These incidents have concerned prejudice against Catholics. So, we are going to commence boxing training, because primarily it is a good and manly sport, and for no other reason,' he says.

We file into one of the classrooms. The desks have all been cleared back against the walls. Brother Brian and the other brothers go up to one end of the room. He holds up some boxing gloves.

'You need to sort out once and for all which is your left hand and which is your right hand. If your right hand is your best hand then you will be leading with the other hand. If you are left-handed, and your left hand is your best hand, then you will be leading with your right hand. Have you got that?'

We all nod like mad, because no one dares say to Brother Brian that they don't understand, in case he takes you out in the front and gets sarcastic. He did that once with Bobby Older, and he cried and everyone teased him in the playground for ages.

There aren't enough gloves to go around, so the little kids, which includes me and John, have to sit around the side and wait while the big kids have a go. They all line up in two rows, all ready to start smacking each other around. Jimmy O'Donnagh even sneaks in a punch on Johnny Dowsett when no one is looking.

Brother Brian looks up and down the rows. 'You are going to do footwork.'

You could see everyone look all disappointed. Footwork is for girls who learn dancing, not for real eight to twelve-year-olds who want to fight.

Daniel Graham from over the road is in the boxing class, even though he is a bit older than us. He started off going to Miramar North, when his father put his foot down and said there was no chance of any of his boys getting brainwashed by bloody Tykes and their

Pope. That lasted until he had to cope with a wildcat strike on the wharves. Little Daniel came home, proudly waving the flag his teacher had given him.

'What the bloody hell's that?' his dad shouted.

'We have to understand all the people of the world, and how we are all the same!' Daniel was telling his father what the teacher had told him.

'Never mind that shit. That's a bloody Russian flag. Bloody Commies. Friggin' pinkos.'

'What's that mean, Daddy?'

'It means, starting Monday, you are a pupil at the Catholic school.'

'What are you doing with my flag, Daddy?'

'Ripping it up and sticking it in the rubbish tin. What I should be doing is sticking it right up your teacher's arse!'

'Why would you do that Daddy!'

'Go out and play!'

'It's raining!'

'You're a kid. Go and smash something!'

Smash. 'Jesus Christ! I never meant it!'

'But you said . . .'

'Never mind what I said! Have you ever thought about leaving school early and getting a job on the wharves, like tomorrow?'

'But I'm only five.'

'Not a problem.'

I am sitting on the side, watching Daniel Graham and the big kids doing their boxing. Then, just when it is our turn, Brother Brian says we have had enough boxing for today and it's probably a good idea if we veer towards learning something from the academic syllabus. He looks really hard at the teachers when he says that.

I go home and don't say anything. I sort of hide out down at the back of our section. I don't know what's going wrong and I'm starting to get frightened. Mum wants to know what's happening, but I won't say. It's all too big. I told Brother Brian that Terry Taylor and James Wilson called us Catholic dogs. Now the whole school is learning boxing. I hope they don't make the whole school come up here and gang up on Terry Taylor and James Wilson. I should have told Brother Brian we called them Proddy dogs, and they both play in our street cricket games. So they don't have to kill them.

I am sure I will never get any sleep again, ever in my whole life. I sneak into the house, hoping to slip quietly into bed, without anyone noticing me. There isn't a chance. Mum is standing there looking at me. My brother John is standing behind her, smiling. I go from trying to be sneaky to angry. Somehow or other he has got there first, and it is all going to end up my fault. I take a breath and get ready for big trouble, and vow I will get even with my brother later on.

'I hear they were doing boxing.'

I wait for more. Nothing.

'Um, yes.'

'Is this because of that business in Newtown?'

'Eh?'

'Three Catholic boys ended up in hospital, because they were beaten up when they were walking on their way home.'

'Eh?'

'If anyone yells at you, or does anything like that, you will tell me, won't you?'

John is behind her, pulling faces at me and shaking his head. It is very confusing, trying to figure out what his mix of signals means. I have a guess and decide he hasn't told her about Terry Taylor and James Wilson. The best thing is not to say anything. So I don't.

'Homework, and then bed!'

'Can I listen to the serial on the radio?'

'We'll see, after the homework.'

John gives a huge smile. It is going to be all right. Everything in the whole world is going to be fine after all. The only thing that is a bit of a worry is that game against Miramar North. They are a bigger school than us, and they've got more kids to pick from. That means they might have a better team, but we don't dare lose, because James Wilson and Terry Taylor will never let us have peace at the bus stop for the rest of our lives. I was smiling. Not now. We have to win no matter what.

chapter thirteen

Brother Brian was also giving thought to the subject of Catholics and Protestants. It was on Wednesday morning the boxing lessons day. The boys were loving it. But then, youngsters given a licence to scrag and rough each other surely would. He might have to do a bit of quiet talking to one or two of the fathers.

He'd heard one of them, Mr O'Byrne, telling a fat young would-be seminarian, whom he was training to be a boxing coach, saying, 'Don't worry about God or anything else. These little children are going to be fighting godless Anglican bastards. Get their left jabs going, and we should have the bastards' teeth spread out all over the road.'

He was doing this in front of us, his class of young boxers, including me. For Brother Brian this was bad. The next bit was worse. Mr O'Byrne, obviously seized by an enthusiasm he could never muster in a day-to-day life administering the debtors ledger for the Department of Tourism and Publicity, started yelling, 'You know what buggering Anglicans means, don't you? No! All right. We'll start with something simpler. What you do when you've got the bastards' teeth all over the road. It makes them concentrate on what they've been doing to Catholics for . . .'

'Thank you, Mr O'Byrne,' Brother Brian broke in, clapping his hands.

'That will be enough for today.'

One of the big boys put his hand up. Brother Brian nodded his permission to speak. 'But we've only been going ten minutes, Brother!'

'I appreciate that, but there's been a mistake. That will be enough for today. I apologise but there is nothing I can do about it.'

There was a groan of disappointment. Brother Brian turned to Mr O'Byrne. 'I was wondering if we might have a few moments to talk?'

'Of course, Brother. I am very keen on this, and I think I can make a real contribution.'

Brother Brian and Mr O'Byrne went off to the

headmaster's office. We never saw Mr O'Byrne again.

Dad was asked to help, even though he had been a wrestler, not a boxer. 'Don't worry about it, Kevin,' the big Marist Brother had said. 'We're teaching them to defend themselves, not to try and win the world championship or anything. Any help you can kick in would be much appreciated.'

'Kicking's about what it would be.'

'Don't worry about it, Kevin,' the big brother said.

But Dad couldn't go. He was busy in the middle of Miramar Park, just at the back of the Film Unit, where he had been working as a bookkeeper. They had a small flagpole set up in the middle of the soccer field, and they were running a New Zealand flag up and down it. A cameraman was lying on the ground, pointing his camera at the flag as it went up and down, dozens of times.

This was the very last act of the 1950 Commonwealth Games in Auckland, but it was several months after the official finish. The crew had been in Auckland and filmed the closing ceremonies, with the important people being all dignified and everything. They filmed the dramatic way the flag was lowered, to symbolise the Commonwealth Games going off to another country. Later, when they were processing the footage, they realised the sun had been directly behind it, and it shone down the lens and prevented them getting the flag on film.

There had been a lot of angry talk about amateur night at the Film Unit and how if there wasn't a New Zealand flag caught on film being dramatically lowered, the lessons of Adolf Hitler would be applied to Film Unit staff. Gas ovens and mass death would be involved. So Dad ended up holding the flagpole. By then no one was worried that it was the wrong sort, that the proper flag was much bigger and that there was a Wellington, not an Auckland, sky behind it. There had been fluffy little clouds in Auckland on the day the Games closed, Dad pointed out, and there weren't any fluffy little clouds in Miramar.

The cameraman was a fraction stressed, because he said to Dad, 'Stick your fluffy little clouds right up your fluffy little bum!' If anyone said that to us in the playground it would have started a fight. Dad just laughed and they all went off to do the filming. Adults were different.

There had only been about six boxing lessons before the Anglican and Methodist ladies turned up at Father Bannon's house.

Father Bannon later told Dad that he guessed they were all in their forties, and that the cost of their clothes would have kept the Miramar parish running for a month.

Once they had all sat down in the small study, the three of them looked at each other, to see who would start. Mrs Sally Manmurray, who lived on the highest part of Seatoun Heights in a huge house above the harbour, was in charge. She was always in charge, because her husband was the senior partner in a long-established and deeply conservative law firm.

— It's the boxing Father. We've been hearing that

since the boxing lessons started over at Marist Miramar, there have been a lot of incidents.

Father Bannon frowned. If this lineup of too-prosperous Anglicans thought they were going to get him to stop the boxing they could whistle *Dixie*, or *Kevin Barry*.

— We were hoping you might see your way clear to perhaps, ah, reducing the frequency of the lessons!

— Mmm. I do want to help, of course, because we all want to see the children thrive and prosper. But the boxing was started after attacks on young Catholics.'

Mrs Manmurray was ready for that one. — That happened in Newtown, not here.

— These things happen everywhere, Mrs Manmurray. I will see what I can do.

Father Bannon stood up to indicate the interview was over. The three women had no choice except to stand up too. Father Bannon was slightly irritated to find he was shorter than all of them.

— I will talk to Brother Brian, and to the Bishop, and see if there is anything we can do.

The women all smiled thin, disappointed smiles at him as they were herded towards the front door. As soon as the door was closed behind them, Father Bannon did a little leap of joy, and threw his hands in the air. He had waited all his life to hear that: Protestants complaining because gangs of Catholics were forcing them to flee in terror. He had never seen that in Northern Ireland, ever. Now, after crossing the world, it was a dream coming to life right in front of him. If those three biddies with their lawyer husbands thought they were going to stop the boxing, they had parted company with any sense of reality. He reminded himself to encourage Father Reilly to beef up that sermon of his. Anglicans scattered in fear. That was the very thing. Oh my, this was a fine, fine day, even if a southerly was ripping wind and rain in all over Wellington.

The three women stood outside. This had not gone well.

Fiona Richardson spoke first. — Shall we try the nuns?

Jane McCampbell looked over at the nuns' house. — Do you think that would be any good? Don't these people take vows to stick together or something.

— That's the Freemasons. You should know — isn't your Fred a Grand Dragon or something.

— I don't know. He just goes off every Tuesday with his little case and squares and aprons and things. It's all a bit silly if you ask me. I only go along to the ball every year because I have to.

— Perhaps it's the same for Catholics!

— Well, come on, said Fiona. — Let's give it a try!

They marched across the road to the door of the nuns' house and knocked. A nun opened the door. — We would like to see the head nun.

The nun looked out and past them, making sure there weren't any men. She did not say anything, just stood aside so they could come inside.

Sister Ignatia had heard the knocking and was coming to see who was there. Introductions done, she asked Sister Angelus to make a pot of tea and to bring biscuits for their guests.

Fiona Richardson decided she was going first, with or without Sally Manmurray's blessing. — It is the boxing at Marist Miramar. We have been having, and I am not exaggerating, some very enthusiastic bands of young Catholic gentlemen looking for Protestant children and attacking them.

— And Methodists and Presbyterians! Jane McCampbell chipped in. Neither of her friends took any notice of her.

Sister Ignatia pursed her lips. — There were some incidents of Catholics being attacked . . .

Fiona was back on familiar ground. — But not in Miramar or Seatoun. We are trying to find out if there are any boys going in for that sort of thing. If we find them, we'll try and help them stop.

Sister Ignatia managed to keep the smile from reaching her face. She would be terrified if she was the adolescent boy having to explain to someone as magnificent as Fiona Richardson why he had done something wrong. — I can talk to the Reverend Mother.

— Will that help?

— The Bishop is not a man who looks for fights with the Reverend Mother. She is a wonderful woman, and dedicated to ensuring the best for the order and for people in general, and the Bishop respects that.

Sally and Fiona sat back, a fraction more relaxed. They understood the concept of powerful men living in fear of the women around them, and that Sister

Ignatia was telling them that although the Bishop ruled he was frightened of the Reverend Mother.

Jane looked around, puzzled. She was finding all this too subtle and complicated. Surely the priests could get the little Catholic bastards to behave like humans and leave everyone else alone? The sooner everything got back to the natural order of things the better. But if anyone was going to get beaten up then surely it ought to be Catholics or Chinese. Wasn't that the real reason they had been brought into the country?

Fiona smiled. — We would be grateful if you could talk to your Reverend Mother.

Sister Ignatia smiled. — We don't want any trouble. Heaven knows we've had a world war and we are supposed to be living in a whole new era. But we are still dealing with men . . .

The three women understood. Sister Ignatia would try, but they shouldn't expect too much.

chapter fourteen

This part of the story took a long time to piece together, and it might still be slightly imperfect, but it is worth telling because a lot of other changes and effects flowed from Father Reilly's sermon. The story drifted together in small individual servings from the priests' housekeeper, from the various policemen who came through our house, from parents who lived close to the priests and who saw more of them than we did. More of it came out over nights of good food and good company, when Father Bannon was relaxed and happy and forgot about us, the little tape recorders sitting quietly in the corner, fascinated by the adults' talk.

As Father Bannon later told it, he was only doing his best to steer the poor confused wretch of a curate, obviously in his hour of great need, back to the path of the Way of the Lord. It didn't quite work out that way.

It all began on the Monday after the three Protestant women met with Father Bannon and then Sister Ignatia. Father Reilly was back in his room after suffering through a two-hour meeting with Father Bannon, Brother Brian and Sister Ignatia. He was tired and restless. Father Bannon in particular had droned on and on and on about the bigotry and the oppression of Catholics in Belfast. God spare them all. Father Reilly had been brought up with all that, and he couldn't wait to get out of Ireland. When they asked for men willing to go to New Zealand he'd answered the call.

Most of his research had consisted of reading a *National Geographic* which contained wonderful pictures of mountains and Maori doing hakas. He'd been very impressed by them, strong and proud and virile. He had looked forward to the idea of bringing light and wisdom to these savage people. When he'd arrived it turned out to be more like working in suburban England, what with Father Bannon refusing to stop talking.

It had been like that in the meeting they'd just left. Father Bannon had dominated everything, long after the other three had started wriggling and squirming with impatience.

When the meeting finally ended, with everyone agreed it was a good idea to teach the boys boxing, and to make sure the girls knew where to get help anywhere in Miramar, he had come back to his desk.

Father Bannon sat down beside him. — What are you doing?

— It is a sermon about bigotry and prejudice.

— Good, good, good. Let's see.

Father Reilly was not keen to show him the draft, but he had no choice. Father Bannon reached over and took the sermon, put on his glasses and slowly read it. Father Reilly suspected this had an element of show business about it, to remind him of the older priest's importance.

Eventually he got a response. — It's the right sort of thing, but isn't it a little bit on the milk and water side? It could do with a few potatoes in the pot, Father.

Father Reilly was left open-mouthed. He thought it was already bordering on the excessively inflammatory. By then Father Bannon was gone, striding away with all the majesty he could manage. Unfortunately he was only five foot three and was losing the battle to grow a respectable moustache, both these things frustrated the air of awe-inspiring moral authority he was keen to cultivate.

Father Reilly looked at the strutting little figure as it disappeared down the corridor. — Why thank you, Father, now there's a very good idea! he snarled to himself. He bent back to his piece of paper, struggling with a sudden anger and indignation. He looked in the cupboard. There was some whisky left. He poured a three-finger glassful and tipped it straight back.

— Aaaagggh! The rawness of the whisky always forced a howl from him, then its warmth spread out through his capillaries calming him. That was better. Now, he would show that pompous little Father Bannon, and the bastard Protestants, who did and who didn't have the fire of the Church about him. Father Reilly would write and deliver a sermon no one would forget. He began to write as he had never written before.

Another whisky! — Aaaaaagggh! That was better. The anger was beginning to settle now. The whisky's warmth raced down now-smooth paths out to the far reaches of his body. Waves of relaxing pleasure radiated over him. He was beginning to feel all right.

Now for the sermon. It would be strong. It would have real impact. It would be magnificent.

An hour later he had written a first draft. He looked over it. If this didn't stir the faithful then nothing would. If godless Protestants were going to abuse and terrify good Catholics then the Catholics were going to make a stand, right here in Miramar. He, Father Reilly, would be the one to voice their thoughts.

chapter fifteen

At 10.30 on the following Sunday morning, a snorting and glaring Jimmy Cassidy walked up to the Anglican Church. He started when he yowled out, — I've come to get rid of the Protestants! My God and my priest have told me to do it, and I am going to save Catholicism.

Most of the congregation knew Jimmy Cassidy. They were used to seeing him wandering around Miramar, talking to himself, his feet bare in both winter and summer. Everyone agreed poor Jimmy was a sad case, and someone should help him, and the doctor and the government should do something about it.

This particular morning no one was worried about the government. They were too busy agreeing it was the moment to get themselves and their children far away. Jimmy Cassidy was holding a large can of petrol and a Zippo cigarette lighter.

As soon as the 9am Mass finished, with Father Reilly's sermon about the evils of religious hatred by Anglicans against Catholics, Jimmy Cassidy had walked down to the petrol station and bought the can and the petrol. That took all his money so he stole the lighter from a display on the counter. Now he was standing at the back of the Anglican church. No one was dismissing him with pity and indifference. Jimmy Cassidy had their undivided attention.

It was enough for the vicar to forget his sermon about adultery, the one subject guaranteed to keep his congregation quiet and attentive.

— Are yer going to stop it, Jimmy yelled at the top of his voice.

All he got in return was the silence of fear and shock.

— I have got to scourge Miramar from the horrors of racial prejudice. Catholics are being attacked by you bastards, he screamed. — I have to burn the fear from our midst, the horror of bloody bigotry.

He stepped forward, letting people scramble over the pews on either side of him. He hurled some petrol over the altar, splashing some near the vicar. — You're all gonna see ya idols and ya icons of ya religious hatred

burned in a wonderful cleansing fire, like Father Reilly
said it oughta be.

Father Reilly. The vicar might be terrified, but he
made sure he registered that name. If he survived, the
priest would pay for turning this monster on them.

Jimmy faced the altar, his hands high. He did not
see Jerry O'Connell, the Miramar policeman walking
up behind him, his singlet roughly tucked under the
braces holding up his uniform trousers and holding a
police baton in his hand. He did not say anything, just
walked up behind Jimmy and hit him as hard as he
could on the back of his head. Jimmy sagged and
dropping on the floor, the petrol can falling on his chest
and spilling the fuel over his face and into his mouth.

O'Connell kicked the petrol can away. Jimmy's
tongue was poking out and he was still. O'Connell was
not interested. — Bloody prick. Man's trying to sleep
on a Sunday morning.

The vicar rushed up behind O'Connell, noticing a
strong smell of beer on the policeman's breath, but
decided this was not the time to mention it. The
parishioners who had escaped had blitzed Wellington
Central with demands for the police. A car full of them
was pulling up. Four uniformed men jumped out,
pulling their helmets on and drawing their batons.

A smiling Jerry O'Connell was walking out. —
You're a bit late. I stopped 'im. I can look after the crime
out this way.

The sergeant pushed him aside. He took one look at
Jimmy Cassidy and yelled for a constable to find a
phone and call for an ambulance. He turned to

O'Connell. — For Christ's sake, Jerry, get away and eat some peppermints so they can't get a whiff of anything on your breath!

— All right, but that — he pointed his baton, with bits of Jimmy's hair on it, at the man on the floor — is what I call a bloody nice bit of baton work.

— Of course it is, but get going.

O'Connell lumbered off towards the Miramar Police Station.

The vicar was beside them. — I have to ring up too.

— Of course Vicar. You want to ring your wife.

— No, the diocesan lawyers.

The sergeant frowned. This was not looking promising. Perhaps he should get on the phone to Mick Mahon. If Anglicans were getting lawyers, Catholics would be getting the worst of it. Naturally, there was always the chance of a perfect result. If Jimmy died, the whole mess might go away without too much fuss.

The ambulance drivers were loading Jimmy into the back of their vehicle when the sergeant got through to Mick Mahon at home.

— Shit! What's that vicar saying?

— That the local priest put him up to it.

— Shit. Don't let anyone get near the priest. Keep the detectives busy finding witnesses and that sort of thing.

— I'll see what I can do.

Two minutes later the phone was ringing in Father Bannon's study. Five minutes after that Father Bannon was calling Father Reilly a fool. Relations between the two priests had begun a free fall.

We did not hear about this till later on Sunday. Our Uncle Pat Conlin turned up at our house and, as he always did, started his visit by wanting to play soccer with all the kids. Mum was never very sure whether it was a good idea to have him around us, because of all his bookmaking and loan-sharking and slygrogging and anything else he did.

Us kids liked him. He was great with us. All he ever wanted to do was get rid of his big, dark suit coat, which he wore in both winter and summer and run round playing soccer. Even though he was in his street shoes, tie and white shirt he was decided he would be Stanley Matthews, the Blackpool winger. He was hopeless at soccer and we would always be able to run right round him and score goals as if he wasn't there.

The other thing he liked was to do favours for the people around him. There was the man in the little green Austin car, he used to try and get us kids to go for rides with him. We were warned never to get in the car with him, because he always wanted to do things he wasn't supposed to do. Uncle Pat heard about this. Next day he arrived with some of his bookie workers and went round to the man's house. They all had a cup of tea and a talk. Next morning the man loaded everything he owned in his little green car and drove off. We never saw him again. A story went round later that no one else ever saw him again.

After the soccer game, when everyone thought we were all out playing I heard Uncle Pat talking to my mum and dad. 'The business is still going, but I've got to face facts. It's pretty well stuffed now. It was good, but it's got too complicated now. There's too many coppers with their noses in it now.'

Dad was nodding and being sympathetic and offering Uncle Pat some of the beer from his flagon. Mum was frowning at this, because it hadn't even reached lunchtime. Dad got a bit embarrassed and looked the other way, but he still drank the beer, and so did Uncle Pat.

'There's also people getting knocked around now.'

Mum looked at Uncle Pat. 'The man they found in Evans Bay?'

Uncle Pat went a bit red, and had another quick glass of beer. 'Um, yeah. That sort of thing.'

Dad looked at her, as if to say, 'Shut up, this is men's talk.'

Mum wasn't taking any notice of that. She was looking at Uncle Pat. 'Did he have a wife and children?'

Uncle Pat was looking ever redder now. 'Um, yeah. I think he might have had, yeah.'

She was holding the flagon. They weren't going to be getting any more beer till she was ready. 'Is anyone looking after them? What will they do about paying their bills and keeping their house, and getting the kids into school and everything?'

Uncle Pat shuffled in his seat. It was the first time I had ever seen him looking anything except completely in control. But he wasn't going to say anything tough to Mum, because the last time he did that, which was about a year before, he wasn't allowed to play soccer or cricket with us, or drink beer with my dad for ages.

'I'm sure someone will be able to help them.'

'A bit?' Mum said, still looking at him.

Dad was getting embarrassed. 'Look, steady on, Colleen. Pat just came up here to visit.'

Mum didn't take any notice of that. 'I hope "a bit" will turn out to be quite a lot, because she's a widow with kids and it won't be easy to find anyone who'll take all that on!'

All Uncle Pat could do was nod.

Dad looked around and saw John and me standing there. 'You kids go outside and play, right now!'

John took off. I went too, so they would hear two lots of footsteps in the hallway. Then I tiptoed back. I wanted to hear what they were talking about. Uncle Pat was saying there was a way to get them, and I don't know who 'them' was, a few thousand quid, which would get their mortgage cleared up. Then he said, 'Poor Frank, it's a shocking thing, and I hope they catch the murderers.'

Mum said she had other things to do, and left Uncle Pat and Dad sitting very quietly.

I listened as carefully as I could, to hear if Uncle Pat and Dad said anything else but all they said was how tough it was trying to make a living when no one was honest any more, and that something called the TAB was going to wipe the business out anyway. Maybe it was time to grab the money and get out.

Dad didn't say anything. He just sat there, drank the beer, and let Uncle Pat talk.

chapter sixteen

The next day, Monday, John and I found out that Jimmy Cassidy might have killed one of the Anglicans, at least indirectly. An old lady who had been in the church died. She got home. She had pains in her chest and rang a taxi to take her into Wellington Hospital. She died in its back seat just as it went up the hill from the Kilbirnie shops.

The newspapers did not have anything about all this. The police had not told them. The Catholics were not keen to rush to tell reporters, and the Anglicans were too busy with looking after the shocked parishioners.

Jimmy Cassidy was in hospital, in a coma, under police guard. If he woke up they were going to charge him with attempted arson and attempted murder.

There were already rumours that Jerry O'Connell was going to be nominated for a medal for his bravery in stopping Jimmy.

John and I were not too worried about any of this. We were too busy hiding behind a car, trying to dodge the stones the three Scots College boys were throwing at us.

'Catholic bastards!' They were all older and bigger than us. One of them fired a stone at us, hitting John on the side of the head. Blood appeared from under his school cap.

I yelled, 'You hit him and he's bleeding.'

'Good. That's why we're chucking stones at him!'

They trapped us there for nearly half an hour. Every time we put our heads up another stone flew past. They were too accurate to risk making a run for it. Our bus had gone. We were definitely going to be late for school. Mum must have heard John screaming out, because she came out and saw the Scots boys and told them to stop. They yelled out at her, 'We're not taking any notice of Catholic dogs.'

Mum went back inside the house.

About five minutes later Mrs Manmurray scorched up in her Jaguar car. She stopped in the middle of the road and walked over to the Scots boys. One of them was her son. 'You, come here, now!'

She was much more impressive than any of the sergeants we used to see in the war movies, and she got faster results. As soon as she shouted, the war was over.

Mum came out. 'Thank you very much.'

'Thank you for helping out with the orphanage bring-and-buy. You,' she snapped at her son. 'You apologise to Mrs Edwards, right now!'

'But she's a Catholic!'

Her voice could cut its way through steel, the road and all the houses. 'Apologise!'

'I am sorry.'

'Better!'

'I am very sorry and nothing like it will happen again.'

'That's a fraction better!'

I didn't know Mum was helping the Anglican women with their bring-and-buy sale. Anglicans were the enemy. They threw stones at us.

Mrs Manmurray was glaring at her son. 'You can apologise to Denis and John.'

'No!'

'What?'

'Sorry.'

'That's a bit more like it. Let's have a look at that cut. I think a plaster might do it.'

Mum looked at it too. John said he felt like a frog in a science experiment, with everyone looking at him that closely.

Mum got a plaster and put it on John's cut. Mrs Manmurray opened the car door and waved me and John into the back seat. 'I'll get them to school.'

'What about us? We don't want to be driving around with Catholics in the car.'

'Get in!'

He looked at his mum. He decided to get in. The other two Scots boys crammed in. They tried to make it as uncomfortable as they could by digging in their elbows. John reached over and grabbed the one nearest him by the top lip and twisted it as hard as he could. The Scots boy yelped with the pain, but moved over to give us more room.

Mum and Mrs Manmurray were standing by the car. I heard them saying something about lawyers and sedition, and how it wouldn't affect the women because the Anglican ladies would help out with the Catholics' rapid-raffle prizes, and that it was just all men being stupid.

John and I weren't worried about that. We were huddled together in the corner of the back seat of the car hoping Mrs Manmurray would hurry up and get going, because the Scots boys were glaring at us, and making us scared. I wasn't sure John's pinch was going to be enough to hold them off for much longer.

'Catholic dogs.'

I thought the only thing I could do was fight back, so I said, 'Proddy pigs.'

They all looked pretty angry then. I wasn't sure our boxing lessons were going to be enough to save us, if a big fight got started in the car.

'Catholic dogs!' Only this time it was a bit louder.

I was just going to yell 'Proddy pigs!' when Mrs

Manmurray got in the car. 'What were you talking about?'

We all said, 'Nothing,' which was safer than starting another fight.

'I thought that's what I heard,' she said and started up the car.

After she dropped us all off at our schools, Mrs Manmurray drove home and spent the morning on the phone. We found out later she was ringing another mother in Johnsonville, who could hardly talk on the phone because her daughter was playing the violin and as there were only two rooms in the house, there was not much privacy. Then she rang Jane McCampbell and Fiona Richardson, and they rang their husbands. By noon she was all finished with everything she wanted to do. She sat down and made herself a sandwich and a cup of tea, and waited.

By 2.30 things had begun happening. Monsignor Grafton was opening a hand-delivered envelope in the Catholic Bishop's house, which was also the headquarters for the Catholic Church in Wellington.

— Fucking hell. He picked up the phone.

Father Bannon answered. — This is Monsignor Grafton!

— How are you, Monsignor? said Father Bannon in a conciliatory tone.

— I am deeply, deeply angry. If I get near you or that idiot of a curate I'll cut both your throats.

— You've heard about the sermon?

— Yes, I have heard about the sermon. I have heard about the petrol. I have heard about the lighter. I have heard about that simpleton being arrested. I have also heard about something else. I have a letter here telling me a group of Anglican lawyers are investigating pursuing an action for sedition against Father Reilly.

— Oh.

— So you are getting the idea.

— Is there anything you want me to do?

— No! You've done quite enough.

Mrs Manmurray's husband rang her at home. A letter had been delivered to the Bishop's house, into the hands of a chap named Grafton, who seemed to be important enough to matter. Mrs Manmurray wrote down the name Grafton, then asked her husband when he would be home. He would be late, at a legal conference and seminar. He had been to these before. There always seemed to be a lot of young secretaries at these seminars, but for the moment she had other things on her mind.

Her next phone call was to Sister Ignatia, at the nuns' house beside Holy Cross School. That started the thing. Now it was time to get more people on the dance floor.

It happened immediately. The next phone call was from Sister Ignatia to Monsignor Grafton.

— It is Sister Ignatia here, from Miramar.

— Of course, Sister Ignatia. Normally we hear from you through the Reverend Mother. But how can I help you?

Monsignor Grafton was careful to mention the Reverend Mother, who he regarded as a saintly woman with a sometimes-too-sharp tongue, and who was serious about being consulted on anything and everything concerning her order.

— I have had a call from a Mrs Manmurray, who wants to talk to me, and only me. She tells me it is just possible she can ask her husband to take a different view.

Monsignor Grafton had the letter threatening sedition in front of him. It was signed by a John Manmurray. This was getting very, very complicated.

— I want you to phone her back and make an appointment for Thursday or Friday. Then I want you to come in here tomorrow and talk about this. This has to be delicately handled.

— Of course, Monsignor. I am sure you will know exactly what to do.

She made no effort to hide the sarcasm. The Monsignor sensed he was helpless, that somehow the battlefront had passed him by.

The Monsignors might have troubles. I don't think they are anything compared to mine. The real problem is Terry Taylor and James Wilson. They've stopped calling us 'Catholic dogs' or anything like it. They've started just walking past us in the morning, smiling as if there is something they know and we don't, and making sure we can see them.

This started out being irritating. Now it is getting towards being scary. Anything would be better than the silence and those sly grins of theirs. We try asking other Miramar North kids if something special is going on. Either no one knows or they aren't telling us.

We try to get our sister Jane to see if the girls who go to Miramar North School will find out anything. She said they don't know what the boys are doing and they all don't particularly care.

Jane has failed us. She is immediately sentenced to not being allowed to play in our games for the next two days.

She goes off and complains to Mum, who tells us we have to let Jane play or she will see what our dad is going to say about it when he gets home. We have to give in. It's too much firepower for us.

John and I put up with Terry Taylor and James Wilson's smirking politeness for nearly three days. It is getting too much. By now they have started refusing to even talk to us about anything.

The final proof that they are plotting something comes on the weekend, when we are lining up a street soccer game. They say, 'Thank you, but we aren't interested in playing.'

That is a first! It also stokes up our curiosity.

Things fall our way on the very next day. James Wilson's sister Janice wants to see if Jane's dolls have a blue-and-white pinafore dress. She wants one for a doll display they are doing at Miramar North School. Jane says she will swap her dress if Janice tells her what is happening.

Jane comes down to where we have decided on a game of cricket, even though it is winter and we are supposed to be playing soccer.

'I want to play.'

'All right. You can be a fielder. You go over there to long-on.'

'No, I want to be a bat.'

'John's batting, and he isn't out yet.'

'You said I could play if I wanted.'

'That doesn't mean batting whenever you like.'

'I know what James Wilson and Terry Taylor are doing, and you don't.'

'What!'

'I want to be a bat.'

'We'll let you bat when you tell us.'

Jane has heard that one before. 'I'll tell you after I've had a turn at batting.'

'All right then.'

'But I'm not out yet.'

'C'mon John. We have to find out what Terry and James are up to.'

'All right, but I keep batting when she is finished.'

'Thank you John. At least someone around here is a gentleman.'

I bowl. 'Howzat! You were out!'

'I never hit it, and it hit me on the leg, and it never hit the wickets!' she wailed.

'That's out, leg before wicket! Your innings is finished. What are Terry and James doing?'

'I'm not out till I've scored a run.'

'Those aren't the rules!'

'They are now. If I don't get a run then I'm going back into the house.'

'All right then.'

In the next 18 balls Jane is clean bowled seven times, caught by the wicketkeeper five times, stumped five times and run out without scoring twice and still no sign of a run. Finally, she keeps her eyes open when she swings the bat and accidentally hits the ball. The ball trickles out in front of her, resting two feet away. No fielder dares go anywhere near it until she has safely run across the road. John and I throw our hands up with joy.

Jane doesn't like that. 'Are you being sarky because it took me a long time to score a run?'

John and I suddenly see the possibility of our source of information disappearing back into its world of books and dolls. 'No. Honest, we weren't!' John and I get a surprise, because we said the same thing at the same time.

She doesn't look convinced. The freckles across the top of her little nose wrinkle. Then she tells us, 'Terry Taylor and James Wilson and all the other kids in the Miramar North soccer team are already having practices, and they have got special moves worked out, so they'll beat you 10–0.'

All we can do is stand there. So that's what it's all about. Team practices!

Jane yells out, 'I don't want to play any more!' and runs off up the hill to the house, before we can say we don't want to play with her any more.

This is serious. Last year Marist Miramar caused a big upset in the Miramar Wednesday afternoon competition when we beat Miramar North 3-0. I got two of the goals and I got a special mention at assembly from Brother Brian. I told Terry Taylor and James Wilson about that, and they got angry. Now they are plotting to even up the scores, which means they'll be able to make our lives miserable by boasting at us all winter.

We look at each other. We might only be eight and nine, but we know what we have to do. We'll both end up getting 'Catholic dogs' and 'Losers' all the way to when the cricket season starts.

We have to find out what these secret new plans are, and then make sure that we can do something to stop them getting away with this terrible plot.

chapter seventeen

At exactly 10.15 Sister Ignatia and the Reverend Mother knocked on Monsignor Grafton's door. A voice yelled from the other side.
— Enter!

The Reverend Mother let her smile ride up one side of her face. Her eyes gleamed. — I suspect the good Monsignor is going to be writing something and we will have to wait until he is finished, she whispered to Sister Ignatia.

The Reverend Mother opened the door. There were two chairs set up in front of his desk. Monsignor Grafton was busily scratching a pen across a piece of paper. The two women stood there, measuring the width of his little bald spot.

The Reverend Mother sat down and she nodded at the chair beside her. Immediately Sister Ignatia had arranged herself and her rosary, Monsignor Grafton snapped out, without looking up, — Do sit down. I am nearly finished.

Sister Ignatia dug her fingers together to help keep a straight face. The Reverend Mother looked straight ahead. The two women were sure that if they had caught each other's eyes they would have fallen on the floor laughing. Finally, Grafton looked up. — It's a mess, and I hope we can sort it out.

— We? The Reverend Mother smiled back at him.

— I meant the Church of course.

She purred back at him — As we all do.

— There's one good thing. We've got lawyers. Armies of 'em. He looked at Sister Ignatia. — If it gets difficult with those women, back out of there and we'll move to plan B.

The Reverend Mother asked, with all the innocence she could manage. — Is that something you will be managing?

Grafton frowned. He had had this polite insolence before. He did not like it then and he did not like it now. Unfortunately he had tried cornering her. It always felt like that game with the little ball and the three tin cups. He had always aimed all his concentration down the sights of his intellect and following the ball, sure he was right and would know where to find the ball. He never did, and he could never understand what went wrong. All he ever knew was he had lost, again.

— I will be personally overseeing things, Grafton snapped back.

— Gosh. Really! She said.

Monsignor Grafton ploughed on, ignoring the Reverend Mother, — Sister Ignatia this is only a preliminary meeting. These people can cause a great deal of difficulty and embarrassment to the Church. We want assurances they will stop. Ideally, you give nothing away.

— Ah, the Church's standard negotiating position for dealing with the nuns, purred the Reverend Mother.

Grafton had missed that. He was smug confidence. — You can rely on me, and I will be there to guide you through every stage.

Grafton sat back, secure he had regained control. He looked a picture of comfortable pompousness. The Reverend Mother's mouth tightened. — That is a comfort to us, Monsignor. She said coldly.

The Reverend Mother was standing up, nodding for Sister Ignatia to stand up too. The women turned and were walking to the door. Grafton bounced out from behind his desk. He was supposed to decide when the meeting was over, because he was the senior clergy present. He could at least get to the door first, hold it dramatically open, in a gesture of dismissal.

He was too late. The two nuns had gone.

chapter eighteen

Mum is sitting doing some sewing and darning when she sees Alice McCarthy walking up the path towards our back door. I am keen to hang around and listen, because when Alice McCarthy visits us she always talks about interesting things; her husband, police, and crimes and investigations and things like that.

'I've been at the prison, taking parcels up to the prisoners for the St Vincent De Paul Society,' Alice said, lowering herself into a chair, taking off a shoe and massaging her swollen foot.

'What does Murray think about that?' Mum asks.

'Murray always says the same thing, that it's a waste of time giving anything to anyone in prison except a bullet and a couple of minutes on the end of a rope.'

'Oh dear. What about a cup of tea?'

Mum looks around. John and Jane and I are all standing near the door. We know what she is going to say. 'Out. Out you go and play!'

'You' means all of us. None of us particularly want to go and play. We've started having trouble coming up with new games now that Jane refuses to play Cowboys and Indians. She got fed up with being the squaw and getting tied to the tree, while the warriors, John and me, run round and have all the fun. Jane is waiting to see what happens next. If anyone says anything about getting tied up, Indian squaws or settlers driving west in covered wagons she will be off back inside, and with a good excuse to stay there.

John has another plan. 'Do you think you can find out more about Miramar North's soccer team?'

She smiles. This is more like it. She seems to have taken to being a spy. 'Yeah.'

'We need to know when they do their practice, and who they have in their team and everything.'

'All right.'

John and I are surprised at that. Surely, it can't be that easy. We expected to have to climb up on roofs, or hide behind trees, and risk our lives like the secret agents in the serials they put on before the main picture at the Saturday afternoon session at the Capitol picture theatre.

'How are you going to find out?'

'I'll ask some of their sisters, I know most of them.'

'But they won't have told girls! This is football stuff.'

'I bet I can find out more than you.'

Our first instinct is to argue. Then we stop. She's already found out about the practices. Perhaps this is a game we don't quite understand, and which we might lose.

'How do we know you will find out proper stuff and not just make it up?' I am still trying to keep control. It isn't much but it is the best I can manage.

'Because I can, and that's that!' she says, folding her arms in front of her and sticking out her lower lip. When she's like that she's a little model of truculent determination.

John and I know there must be a way around that, but we can't think of it right now. Perhaps being spies might be better. Otherwise we could end up having to help Jane with her dolls.

We are right. 'If I find out something, what do I get in return?' she says

I start with the easiest. 'We'll play women's basketball!' We can easily turn that into men's basketball.'No, because you cheat, and don't play properly. I want you to help me with my dolls' house!'

It could be worse. We might have had to sit in the

living room for two hours while she told us all about her dolls, and their life stories and their clothes and everything.

John and I nod at each other. 'All right then.'

She smiles her freckled-nose smile.

John says, 'We better play something.'

'No Cowboys and Indians.'

'What about tag?'

'What about touch rugby?'

'As long as no one gets tied up.'

'It's rugby!'

'All right then.'

We get going on the touch rugby. John gets hacked off. He has ended up playing against the two of us. Unfortunately for him Jane is good at basketball, so she doesn't make many mistakes in catching and passing, and she can run fast. It takes nearly twenty minutes of running back and forward before Jane drops a pass. Because John got the ball away from Jane she has to be on her own. She decides this might not be fun. 'Mum yelled out for me!' she says.

I didn't hear Mum yell out. Neither did John. We can see her — she's inside talking to Alice McCarthy. They are having a cup of tea and some of the biscuits out of the red tin, the one we're never allowed to touch because our arms and legs will be cut off and used for tomato stakes. The window is open and we can hear some of what they are saying. 'It started about a month ago. He can't sleep all through the night. He wakes up screaming, and he is all sweating and he looks horrible.'

'Has he ever been anything like this before?' asks Mum.

'No, not like this. I think something horrible has happened.'

'Is it anything to do with that man they found in Evans Bay? He's working on that case, isn't he?'

Alice nods. 'I think he's off the homosexuals now, too.'

She pronounces it 'harma-six-yools'. 'He's doing terrible long hours, and there's another case they might get him working on. There's a girl, Marie West, gone missing.' She pronounces it 'gawn'. 'She was supposed to be going to a youth club or something, and she's disappeared.'

'Gone up north for a while?'

'Gone up north for a while' is what people say when a single girl gets pregnant and goes away to have the baby. Most of them have it adopted out, usually without ever seeing it. Afterwards they come home and look for a husband. If they are lucky the boy who got them pregnant has gone or has kept his mouth shut, so the girl can pretend she is are still a virgin. If they find a boy who hasn't had much sex there is a good chance he won't know the difference. I know about this because some of the boys at Miramar Rangers Soccer told us juniors all about it. They are eighteen or nineteen, so they know about these things.

'He's a lot more moody now,' says Alice. 'His insomnia's come back and he prowls around the house at all hours of the night.' She looks out the window for a moment. I can see her eyes are wet from tears building up in them.

Mum spots us coming in and whisks us straight through the door into the passageway and closes it behind us. Alice is crying. We can hear her sobs through the door. 'Your kids . . . Lucky . . . so bloody lucky.'

Behind us Jane says, 'Are you going to help me with my dolls?'

She says it loudly enough for Mum to hear. It works. The footsteps are too fast for us. Mum has the door open before we can escape. Jane guessed what was going to happen and has already made a run for it.

'You and you,' she points to me and John. 'Go!'

She waits till we get to the end of the passageway, and then shuts the next door. I glance back, just in case there's a chance of slipping back. None. She stands there like a policeman, making sure I keep going.

chapter nineteen

Sister Ignatia pushed the doorbell. Within seconds the door opened. Sally Manmurray smiled and waved her on into the house. She must have been waiting behind the door. Sister Ignatia had always thought women like this made a point of never appearing to be in a hurry. Sally Manmurray must have been anxious. That was interesting.

Sister Ignatia stepped past and into the house. It was

bigger than it looked from the road, and was beautifully furnished. The walls were painted off-white; portraits of Maori men and women looked out from heavy gold frames. Jane McCampbell and Fiona Richardson were standing, waiting. A tray with a silver teapot and porcelain milk jug, sugar bowl and cups and saucers was sitting on a small coffee table, polished oak with curved legs. Sally gestured for everyone to sit down, and began pouring tea.

— Is tea all right? Or would you like something else? She glanced across at a well-stocked liquor trolley.

Sister Ignatia shook her head. — There's enough of that around Miramar without me starting. The four women nodded sympathetically.

— It was a terrible business, that young man at the Anglican Church, Sally Manmurray said.

Sister Ignatia had been told by the Reverend Mother, — Keep agreeing with them. Otherwise, breathe through your nose. They'll tell you what they want. People always do. You just have to be listening for it.

Sister Ignatia remembered the interview when the Reverend Mother had asked her to take over the little school. She did not want the job. She was too young. She did not have enough experience as a teacher, and none as an administrator.

The Reverend Mother kept listening. Eventually Sister Ignatia began running out of reasons to refuse. Still the Reverend Mother kept listening. She continued to listen while Sister Ignatia began to find a way through her own objections. The Reverend Mother was pleased; Sister Ignatia bathed in the approval. The fight was over. When they were finished, Sister Ignatia had agreed to take over the school, without quite knowing how it happened.

Sister Ignatia nodded sympathetically.

— It is a terrible business.

Sally was watching Sister Ignatia. The nun had not said anything. Either she was young and frightened and did not know what to say, or she was carefully guarding her cards.

— Don't you agree?

— Of course. It is a sad affair. The Bishop is very upset about it all and I think he is hoping there will be a way to help everyone, Sister Ignatia said.

The three Anglican women nodded. Sally looked at the other two. Sister Ignatia felt the atmosphere change. That was quick. This was when she found out what these women wanted.

Sally led off. — There is a Sister Szilvassy in Sydney. Orchestras all round the world take her violin pupils. There are youngsters who have the talent and who work hard and who would be a credit to New Zealand . . . if they had the opportunity.

There it was. Get one of their favourites into Sister Szilvassy's teaching schedule and the problems over Jimmy Cassidy would slide softly away.

— I will have to check with the Reverend Mother.

— Of course. There's the phone there. If you would like to use it? It was an order.

Fiona Richardson stood up. — I want to see your new rhododendrons, she said to Sally.

As soon as they were gone Sister Ignatia dialled.

In the kitchen Fiona heard the extension telephone 'ping' and out of force of habit reached for the receiver. Sally lightly tapped her hand in rebuke. Fiona shrugged and allowed herself to be shepherded out into the garden. They would be able to see Sister Ignatia from there.

The phone on Monsignor Grafton's desk rang. The Reverend Mother and the Bishop were sitting on the other side of the desk. It was what they had been waiting for, the conversation between the three of them having petered out into a moody silence.

Grafton reached for the receiver. The Bishop reached it first.

— Walker.

— It is Sister Ignatia here.

— What do they want?

— They have given me a list of three young violinists they would like enrolled with Sister Szilvassy.

— Ye gods. That's in Sydney! What about singers! Tell them to get singers. I can manage singers. We've got singing teachers. Armies of them!

— They are set on violinists.

— Bloody hell. You stay on the line. I'll get the Reverend Mother to put a call through to Sydney.

The Reverend Mother was already crossing the room to another telephone and dialling the number for tolls assistance.

When she nodded to indicate that the Bishop in Sydney was on the line, Walker signalled for her to take Grafton's phone. They crossed in the middle of the room. The Reverend Mother paused for a moment, to make sure who she was talking to. — Ignatia?

— Reverend Mother.

— Where are they?

— Out looking at the rhododendrons.

— Good. Keep them out there.

— How.

— Stand where they can see you, and make sure they can see you are still talking on the phone.

— I can see them. I think it's starting to get a bit cold, and they only have blouses on. They can't be very comfortable out there.

— Don't forget, Ignatia, their husbands are trying to put Father Reilly in prison.

— Is that a completely bad idea?

— I agree, but we are supposed to be all of us on the same side, at least until we get this sorted out. Then the Bishop can sort things out with him.

Bishop Walker was getting red in the face. It was obvious the discussions were not going well. The Reverend Mother could hear the Bishop in Sydney yelling. — Have you got the slightest idea what it is like trying to negotiate with them? Have you any idea how much I am going to have to trade away?

The Reverend Mother waited, trying not to smile. Universality was wonderful. Besides, she had her own problems. — Reverend Mother, they are still out there in the garden and I think it is going to rain.

— Bishop!

— Just a moment, Reverend Mother! The Bishop turned back to give his full attention to the receiver.

A broad Australian accent was powering back at him. — We might be able to squeeze in one kid, but that's all.

— One!

— Take it or leave it!

— I'll take it.

— Don't forget, a favour!

— Our Bishop has talked to the Bishop in Sydney, said Sister Ignatia. — We have been very lucky to get one place with Sister Szilvassy.

Sally Manmurray raised an eyebrow. — One!

— Otherwise the Bishop says it is all over and the case can go ahead. The lawyers can fight it out in court.

The three Anglican women looked at each other. It was a dialogue without words as they nodded and raised their eyebrows at each other. Sister Ignatia held her hands together in her lap, making sure the other three women could not see her fingers were crossed.

Sally smiled. — One pupil would be wonderful, and we are very grateful.

Sister Ignatia half flopped back in her chair with relief. The deal was done.

Sally stood and smiled. The meeting was over. Fiona Richardson rushed past to open the door, all smiles. She beamed at Sister Ignatia. — You know we would have been quite happy just to have got one of our girls in with the singing teacher in Auckland.

That night a girl in Johnsonville was being told that she would spend the next three years in Sydney. If she didn't work like the only stoker on an ocean-going liner, she would be explaining to Sally Manmurray. The young girl felt her mouth go dry. A combination of her own ambition and the prospect of Sally was easily enough to keep her in practice rooms and away from boys for three years.

That night there was another conversation in the Manmurray household. Frank Manmurray had come home grinning. — We've got the tykes by the balls. As soon as we file the sedition papers I think we can get it in front of Manderson. He hates them. He'll have that priest up in Mt Crawford bending over and parting the cheeks of his backside in the search area before he can say, 'The Pope's an arsehole.'

— No you won't.

— Eh?

Sally Manmurray had sat down and talked to him for a long time about what a marriage was supposed to be like, with a husband accepting the support and love of his wife and prospering, and occasionally taking an interest in the things she was doing. Or there was a different sort of marriage. Wasn't she going to be going along to all those receptions, where he was wanting to lobby to be made a judge? If she had a sherry or two more than she should and started telling the other wives about some of his little indiscretions, it would surely get back to the people who picked the judges.

After an hour of this Frank Manmurray suddenly decided he wasn't feeling much like dinner, and that there were things he needed to do back at the office. Sally watched him go, smiling as he scowled back at the house and accelerated down the driveway.

Next morning Frank Manmurray met an icily polite Judge Thomas Manderson to tell him the action for sedition against Father Reilly was being withdrawn. Manderson's lip curled. He was not pleased.

chapter twenty

Dad is feeling he should be doing more with the kids. The problem is, what? It is Sunday afternoon and far too windy and rough to go fishing. One thing that won't be happening is our getting in the car and driving anywhere. This is because Dad and a couple of the other fathers have been having a few beers after lunch, enough to make them nervous about driving anywhere in case they get stopped by a policeman.

Dad is looking at the garden and the paths, to see if there is anything needing fixing. I don't mind this. I am happy to carry tools and be the helper. I know I'm not going to get any decision-making power. The last time I was turned loose to do weeding I had some trouble figuring out what was what, and pulled out a few too many flowers. There had been some unpleasantness over this, and I had been accused of trying to get out of gardening.

'I'm not!'

'Would you be that rough and careless if you were playing soccer?' Dad said.

'Not when I'm playing as a defender. I rip everything down then. The ball might get past me, but nothing else.' I was trying to make the point that my gardening was the same as my defending. Nothing survived.

Jane, curse her eyes, had scored points left, right and centre, by sorting the weeds from the flowers and replanting the flowers. Love and understanding flowed down on her. Jane gave me one of her big freckled smiles and trotted off to remind Mum who had pulled out the flowers in the first place.

That night Jane rubbed it in a bit, when she asked if she could stay up a bit later and listen to the radio. Mum's answer was a smiled, 'Yes, of course.' I was convinced Jane wasn't a bit interested in the radio but was just giving me a reminder I might be the oldest but that it didn't mean a thing. I had to admit I was impressed at how easily a six-year-old could run rings around two older brothers.

That was last night. Now I am following Dad around

the section. 'You have to try to be in control of things, son. You have to get destiny and make it work for you.'

'Yes Dad.' I don't have the slightest idea what he is going on about.

'I've passed the last of my accounting exams. I start a new job on Monday, as an auditor for Civil Aviation.'

'Yes Dad.' I have no idea what auditing, Civil or Aviation are. But if he's happy, I'm happy.

'There's something else that might happen first.'

'What's that?'

He looks down at the road. A priest is getting out of a little car. I have a good look at him, but I don't recognise him. Lots of priests visit our house. They are all adults, which means they all look the same, unless they are women. They have longer hair and wear dresses.

Dad looks down at me. 'I want you to keep playing around the section.'

'Can I do anything I like?'

'As long as you don't break anything!'

I wander off to practise soccer moves on the lawn. No one will stop me continuing on the path to becoming the best soccer player in the world. John is over at one of the neighbour's houses. Jane is at the Wilsons' house, hopefully finding out more about the Miramar North School soccer tactics, but I suspect she's wasting the whole afternoon playing with dolls and not even thinking about our soccer game.

Dad disappears around the front of the house, going in the front door. This is different. Normally he says hello when the priests arrive; and takes them in through the back door with lots of talking and ceremony.

My Mum was in the kitchen putting fruit in bottles for later in the winter.

I think I remember who the priest is, but not his name. He is one of the Redemptorists from the monastery in the city. He smiles at me and keeps walking up the pathway. He must have been to our place before because he knows exactly where he is going.

'Hello Denis,' he says.

He knows my name. Now I have to call him something, and I can't remember his name. The one really good thing about priests is you can always say, 'Yes Father,' and know it will be all right. So that's what I do.

'Bless you, Denis,' he says.

By the time it is my turn to say something he is round the corner and gone, loping up to the back door. I wait for a second and zoom over to the pine trees and climb up one. You can see into the dining room from there. Mum is sitting there, and the priest is on the other side of the table. I can't see Dad. He must be somewhere else.

I am being so nosy because I'm bored with kicking a soccer ball against the fence. I suppose I could improve my soccer if I do that, because you always get better when you practise things. It's just that being the best in the world will have to wait.

Mum is getting the Redemptorist a cup of tea. Adults do that, get each other cups of tea and then talk about not-very-much, before they get to the real stuff. I wonder if they have a book of rules for talking to each other, like the one for the Mass that tells people what to say and when.

I decide I want to hear them. They are still on the tea part, so I scoot down the tree and sneak across to our basement, which is just under the dining room. If I climb up in the joists I can hear what's being said just above me.

The priest is talking. 'Kevin's a terrific Labour man. He's worked hard for the party, and people have noticed it. Plus he's an accountant and that's something they'll need when they go back in. They've got spenders. What they need is bean counters.'

Mum mutters something about Dad turning out to be a good accountant.

'He's a family man too, and that always goes down well,' the priest says.

'Yes,' Mum says, sounding as if she isn't sure where this is going.

'You can get my drift, can't you? I'm saying there's a place for Kevin as the Labour candidate for Miramar. It's his if he'll take it.'

'What about Billy?' Billy Fox is the incumbent member of Parliament.

'The party will look after him. He'll be all right.'

'Won't the Labour Party people want Kev to stand in some other electorate first, so he'll get experience or something, before he goes in a safe seat?' Mum sounds doubtful.

'Well, of course, yes, normally. But it would be a bit different for Kevin, because he'd be such an out-standing candidate they wouldn't worry. And there's

the family. No one would expect him to be away somewhere else campaigning for weeks.'

'That's something.' Mum still doesn't sound
convinced.

'I'm getting the feeling, Colleen, you aren't all that
enthusiastic about all this.'

'Keep telling me about it all.'

'We've had a word with Fintan Walsh. He says there
shouldn't be a problem from the Federation of Labour
end. The unions are all right.'

'Wasn't Billy Fox in the Seaman's Union? That's
Walsh's union, isn't it?'

'Billy's Cooks and Stewards. Fintan's Seamen. It's a
completely different outfit. Just quietly, that might have
something to do with Fintan not being too worried if
Billy gets eased out of the picture.'

'Isn't that difficult to do, get someone who is a sitting
member of Parliament to just step aside?'

'The party's not supposed to do that, but Fintan
could organise it. No trouble at all, and naturally the
Church would be right behind Kevin and yourself. Both
of you are ideal Catholic people; members of the Third
Order of St Francis, hard workers for the Church out
here in Miramar.'

The priest stops. His selling pitch is over.

Mum looks at him. 'You are offering him the
Miramar seat, and that'd probably mean he will be the
member of Parliament forever.'

'He could drive home after work. Not like the others,
who have to live in hotels and flats,' the priest adds.

'And get into trouble.' Mum's tone is sharper.

Even though I can't see them, I can imagine the Redemptorist shrugging his shoulders. I have seen him do that before when he did not want to answer something. 'Of course, there have been problems in Parliament. But they've been with people stranded away from their families. Kevin is different. He'll be home at the end of the day. He's a solid family man.'

'Have you talked to Kevin?' she asks.

There is another pause. The Redemptorist has suddenly realised that Dad might not have talked about this with Mum, but instead talked about it with other people. That could be trouble.

'I can tell you what I think now,' Mum says.

'No, no, no. There's no hurry. Think it over!'

'I don't want him to do it.'

'Look, don't give a firm answer today. There's plenty of time. Talk it through with Kevin.'

'It'll be the same answer.'

'Is it because he didn't talk to you first? It's an accident. We came to him, and it was only yesterday. The poor fellow probably didn't have time, what with all the children, the wonderful children, you have to look after.'

'It's not that. It's Bellamys. It's a pub full of cheap booze and it's open all the time. That's the problem. God, we live out here in a dry area and he still manages to keep drinking no matter what. It would never end if he got in there.'

'I am sure we can get help for him. We can talk to him about taking the Pledge against the drink.'

'I doubt whether that'd help.'

'Don't make a firm decision now. Talk it over. I've got to be running.'

'It's no! It'd be too dangerous.'

I sneak out of the basement and along the side of the house. I go in through the front door and down towards the door that leads to the kitchen. Just as I get there I stop by Mum and Dad's bedroom. The door is three-quarters closed. I hear this funny sound, and peek in. Dad is sitting with his back to the door. He has his head in his hands and his shoulders are jerking up and down.

I have never seen or heard this before. It's my Dad crying.

I stand there at the door. I don't know whether to go up and say anything or not. I've seen Mum crying, and Jane always rushes up and tosses her arms around her neck, but that's girls. I don't know what boys are supposed to do, so I just stand there, feeling helpless. I decide he might not want me to put my arms around his neck, so I tip-toe away.

I'm not sure if it is a good idea to rush up to Mum either, so I just slip back out of the house, the way I came. Once I am outside I go back to the pine tree and climb up high. From there I can see into the dining room. Mum is sitting in the dining room, with her head in her hands. It's hard to tell, but from a distance it looks as if she might be crying too.

It isn't much fun sitting in the pine tree, watching Mum crying and knowing that Dad is just on the other side of the door from her, crying too. I don't know, but when I've seen stuff like that in the newsreels at the Capitol pictures down in Miramar the people who are crying always seem to be cuddling each other.

Maybe it's different in real life.

This is worse than not being fun. It is horrible. It's horrible because they are unhappy and I don't know how to fix it. Everyone is always telling me that I am the oldest, and the 'man' of the family. If this is being the man of the family then I don't think it amounts to much.

chapter twenty-one

I am not the only one deciding that life in Miramar is getting complicated. Brother Brian had two lists in front of him. One was the names of Marist Miramar boys who had been threatened or attacked because they were Catholics. The other was a list of the Catholic boys whom Protestant parents had complained about because they were using their new boxing skills to beat up their sons.

The Catholics getting beaten up were the smallest,

weakest and least athletic. From what he could see of the Protestants it was the same: his pupils were picking on the weakest.

So religion might not necessarily be the driving force. It was boys, on both sides looking for the easiest targets. This could be crushed. It was also a good clue that the days of the Catholic ghetto might not last forever.

Sister Ignatia was crossing the playground, on her way to his office.

— Brian.

— Ignatia.

He sat down behind his desk. This annoyed her, because it was a signal he was the more important. He was no such thing. He could no more say Mass or give the sacraments than she could. Couldn't he keep these little touches for the priests? But there was work to do and she was not going to waste time on challenging this little bit of pompousness.

Both Brother Brian and Sister Ignatia were worried. It was drink. Fathers were drinking too much. There were arguments with their wives. People had been hit. Some had taken it out on the kids. The older ones were taking it out on the younger ones. There had been at least two cases of mothers hitting fathers with flying saucepans and rolling pins. Brother Brian and Sister Ignatia had been right through the rolls of their schools, trying to identify families where either gambling or beer-drinking was affecting daily life. Their estimate was fifteen per cent. Ignatia and Brian had begun by aggressively promoting the idea of non-drinking families, filling the children with anti-alcohol messages, hoping they would shame the parents into not opening the beer, sherry and whisky bottles.

They had approached Father Bannon, to see if he would let fly from the pulpit on the subject of alcohol. The priest had been clear, direct and to the point. 'After the shambles when that idiot tried to set fire to the Anglican church? No. We are going to be having a full year of "God Loves Everyone, Regardless of Religion" from our pulpits. If you want anything wound up in this parish, buy an alarm clock!'

They had taken the fight back to their classrooms. And they were losing.

— No, Brian, we aren't losing. It's just that we aren't winning.

He dropped his chin in his meaty hand. — It's not just the drinking. There's loan sharks going around, practically demanding people take money for betting on horses, and lending them money to pay their debts. They have to let their houses be used for slygrogs, or heaven knows what else.

Sister Ignatia nodded. — And the slygrogs move on as fast as the police find them.

— Or the police don't want to find them.

The local policeman, Jerry O'Connell, despite his Irish name had not been a great deal of help. In fact he seemed to pick on Catholics, making their arrests as rough and public as possible. He had told Brother Brian, — I'm Catholic and it's bloody Catholics who are embarrassing me, behaving like bloody children around the beer. I get sick of being sneered at by all the Freemasons at Central, so I'm out to put a stop to it.

— Beating people up for just having a few drinks too many?

Jerry O'Connell smiled his mean little smirk. — The Protestants? Oh, I'm not as tough on them. Let them think they can get away with drinkin' and wreckin' things. They'll only get more confident and do worse. Then I'll get a hand on their collar and it'll be for keeps. Give the bastards plenty of rope.

Jerry O'Connell was even less likely to change his ground than Father Bannon.

So Brother Brian and Sister Ignatia had fought on, doubling the number of visits to homes, trying to get a sense of the problems. It was always the same, a façade of polite hospitality, undercut with a river of fear.

They would hear repeatedly: — Of course we are pleased to see you. The teachers at the state schools don't do this, and it is wonderful you make the effort. Of course we would let you know if there was anything wrong. If any of ours give trouble at school, you let us know. They won't do it again. It was good to see you. Bye.

As soon as the door close it was, — Thank God they've gone. I need a beer.

— No you don't, you've had enough to drink!

— Don't you tell me when I've had enough.

Brother Brian and Sister Ignatia could tell what happened next. In the playground at lunchtime, children sat quiet and withdrawn, wondering why everyone else didn't have to live in a battlefield. Or others dominated the playground games, looking for attention, being bullies, trying to control their world so no one would hit them again.

— What do we do now? Brother Brian's shoulders were dropped.

— I suppose we keep going, and we pray, and we keep working.

Brother Brian and Sister Ignatia were not the only ones thinking about the problems in Wellington's eastern suburbs. Two days later Jerry O'Connell was at Wellington Central, knocking on Inspector Mick Mahon's office door, being ushered in and gestured to a chair.

Mahon sat opposite him, rather than behind the desk. — What about a drop of something, Jerry?

— No thanks, sir.

— For God's sake!

— Sorry. No thanks . . . Mick.

— That's better.

Mahon sat back, looking at an unusually nervous O'Connell. — What can I do for you, Jerry? You're not worried about that boy who tried to torch off the Anglicans are you? Don't worry. If he lives he's heading for the loony bins. It won't get anywhere near a trial. That'll mean it won't bounce back on that thick bloody priest out your way. You did well though giving the nut a good clip round the ear.

— I just stopped him, that was all.

— You're goin' up for a medal.

— I never did nothin'. I just walked up behind him and smacked 'im one.

— Bloody sight more than anyone else in this police force! Mahon snapped.

He was filling in time, and knew it. Years of dealing with O'Connell had told him he would eventually find out what O'Connell really wanted. Mahon had long since give up trying to speed information's journey through O'Connell's convoluted mental pathways.

— Not having any luck with findin' who cleaned up Frank Wilkins?

Mahon was careful not to let his sigh get past his throat. If this was what O'Connell wanted, then that's what he would be getting. — We got the body. We got Frank's car full of blood and shit. The cheeky buggers used his own car to drive him to Evans Bay and chuck him in, and then dumped it up in Mount Victoria.

— Musta bloody panicked.

— We've even found where he was aced. There's blood everywhere. It's the workshop where Pat Conlin runs his book.

— Jees.

— And now there's this girl missing from up Mount Victoria. That place is getting too much news.

— She a Catholic?

— Yeah. Disappeared going out to Young Christian Workers. There's Catholics all through this thing. I got the Freemasons like rabid dogs, queueing up to get on the case. They'll put someone up on the platform for Frank Wilkins. It'll be an O' someone or other, too.

— How long can you keep a lid on it?

Mahon was getting close to despair. Wasn't O'Connell capable of ever getting to the point. — I'm a police inspector. I don't keep lids on investigations!

— Sorry, Mick. Look, maybe I'd better come back another time.

— No. I'm sorry about all that Jerry. I didn't mean to say that. The work catches up on me sometimes.

Mahon sat back. He was definitely tiring. O'Connell sat opposite him, nervous now and trying to make up his mind whether to just stand up and run.

Mahon decided this was enough. — What's going on, Jerry?

— There's trouble out in Miramar. I've got the brothers and the nuns tellin' me there's a lot of domestic trouble goin' on.

Mahon leaned forward. — Jerry, it's men and women under one roof. There's always gonna be trouble, and there's bugger all we can do about it.

It's getting worse. There's a lot of beatin' up goin' on.

— Is it the bookmakin' and the slygrogs?

— I'd say it was both, Mick. I'd say definitely!

— They are saying there are police mixed up in it. O'Connell nodded.

— Leave that part to me, Jerry. But you get busy out there. Get some arrests. If the nuns and priests get on to the Bishop and he starts whispering in ears there's no knowing where it'll end.

— I know one place I can do quickly.

— Good. You better make sure at least one Catholic ends up in the bag.

O'Connell smiled back. He was happy now. He had said his piece. He stood up to leave. Mahon hefted himself out of his chair. — No batons. We don't want anyone else in hospital, he warned.

By the time O'Connell got his mouth open to protest, the door had closed, leaving him alone in the corridor outside Mahon's office. He shrugged. He was safe. The Catholics knew he was one of theirs and would never shift ground. The Freemasons had discounted him because he was a lowly constable. He could be counted in the enemy ranks and forgotten. Both sides saw him as a tired old warrior out to pasture in the softest of soft spots, Miramar.

But not too tired. Three days later Jerry O'Connell walked into a Strathmore Park house. Three depressed looking men in their fifties, all wearing singlets and cheap trousers, were sitting in a lounge room, disconsolately drinking warm beer. A rough bar was in a corner. The house owner was sitting beside it hoping the other three would do a bit more drinking.

O'Connell piled them all into the back seat of his car and drove them back to his little Miramar Police Station. He was pleased when he found he had got it all just right. Three Protestants and one Catholic.

His wife, a better typist, plugged through the paperwork for him. Then he let them go, bailed to appear in court the next day. He was proud. He was doing his bit to bring peace to Miramar, to drive back the scourge of drink and crime the brothers and sisters were convinced was sweeping the eastern suburbs. He slipped off his uniform jacket and yelled for his wife to bring him a beer. By then the four men were well on their way back to Strathmore Park to the same house, to the same seats in the lounge room and another four bottles of beer.

It was unlikely that O'Connell would raid them twice in one night. But it paid not to take risks. This time they would do their drinking in the dark.

That night a doctor and a nurse checked Jimmy Cassidy's pulse. Nothing. They pricked a pen down his fingernails. Nothing. They squirted ice-water in his ear. Nothing. Then they pulled a sheet up over his face and wheeled him off to the morgue.

Mick Mahon breathed a quiet prayer, joining several other highly placed and not-so-highly placed Catholics in giving thanks to their God that the whole incident was to be buried along with Jimmy Cassidy.

chapter twenty-two

It is always the bus stop where things happen. There he is, Terry Taylor, coming up towards us. John and I get ready for trouble, which could come either way. We could get attacked. Or there would be another lot of those secret little smiles. Last time it was the smile so I am assuming it is going to be the same thing again.

It's not. Just as he gets close to us I see a funny look in his eye, one I have seen in other people. Only by the time I remember where, it is too late. He has dropped into a boxing pose and hit John on the nose. I jump forward, but he hits me in the stomach. I only just get my head out of the way from the uppercut I know is coming next.

He stands there, yelling at us, 'I got ya. I got ya. Got ya. Got ya.' He is jumping with joy, bouncing around like a boxer. 'I got ya, and I'm gonna flatten ya!'

He would do it too, except some adults arrive at the bus stop.

Terry looks around. This is trouble. The chances are that at least one of the adults knows his parents, so he settles for a hissed, 'See, I've been learning to box too. I can beat ya, Tykes.'

He is off, on his way to school. John is left sitting in the bus shelter feeling his nose. 'I think it'll be all right. I never had a broken nose before, so I can't tell if this is broken or not?'

I don't think it is. John has been hit on the nose lots of times when he's been boxing, most of them when I've got him with a straight left, and he has never had a broken nose. He's got a really tough nose.

I am okay. I have been hit in the stomach lots. It gets you winded but not much else. But what is serious is Terry Taylor might have got better at boxing than either of us. If we don't think of something to make his life miserable, he will bully us to death. Banning him from our street games probably won't work. Our mothers will start talking and that'll be the end of that.

We could wait till he comes out to play with us, and then grab the ball and take off. He won't like that. He likes to be at the centre of things. Now that is good, but not good enough. No, the soccer game against Miramar North is the absolute key to this. Marist Miramar has to win both that game and the Wednesday afternoon league.

First things first. If we are to get his compulsory admission to our games cancelled, John and I will have to lobby Mum. We decide it would be best to wait till after dinner, when everyone is fed and relaxed and Tony and Jane are in bed asleep.

Which is what we do.

We sit quietly, really quiet, in case Mum and Dad decide it is our bedtime too. If they do, they are usually unstoppable. Attempts at raising important issues are seen as delaying tactics, and brushed aside.

Mum and Dad are talking. Things do not sound too happy.

'What exactly do you mean, travelling?'

'I am going to be auditing the books on Air Force bases, to make sure the money is being spent properly.'

'I know what auditing is. I want to know how long you will be away.'

'I think it works out to about one week in six.'

'One week in six!' She is being really cool and determined about it. She does not sound like the women Dad sometimes tells us about, who are not very 'logical and not as good at things like accountancy, science and economics'.

'Do you have to stay on the Air Force places?'

'Bases. Yes, but only for about three nights.'

'Do they have hotels there?'

'They are messes.'

'I don't care what they call them. I suppose everyone spends the evening drinking.'

'Some, not everyone.'

Mum stands up. 'Some! Huh!' She goes out into the kitchen and starts to rattle around with the dishes and stuff.

Dad looks at us. 'It's a better job. There will be a bit more money,' he says.

Mum wanted to go to Spain or Europe or somewhere as soon as they were married. She'd wanted to ever since she had a good look at Wellington, and Miramar in particular. Being stuck on top of a hill miles from anywhere is not her idea of fun. Now there are four children. There is still a twenty-minute walk to the nearest shop, and her husband is going to be away for at least one week in six.

Dad follows her into the kitchen. She is saying, 'If that is what you want to do, then I suppose that's the end of it.'

'Look, it's better money. It's a start on a proper career.'

'And you'll be away all the time!'

'Not all of it.'

Not long after that Mum goes into the bedroom and shuts the door. Dad is wandering around, looking lost. He sees us. Judging by the look on his face we can forget bringing up banning Terry Taylor from our games.

'You, and you!' he snaps at John and me. 'Bed!'

He sounds a bit as though he is already in the Air Force, like an officer or something. John and I give up and go off to get our pyjamas and get into our beds. John is cleaning his teeth and he has his face up close to the window. 'I don't think my nose is broken. It looks pretty straight to me. Don't they go crooked when they are broken?'

I don't know. I've never had a broken nose. John is so busy looking at his nose he doesn't notice the washbasin overflowing. I see it first and grab the tap to stop the water. We look at the big puddle of water on the floor. 'Yuck,' says John.

'We'd better clean it up. They aren't in a very good mood.'

John hands me the towels while I mop up and squeeze the water into the bath. There is a lot of water, so it takes longer than we want. In the end we get it all cleaned up. Now all the towels are wet.

'Whoops!' I say.

John has a good idea. 'What about folding them back neatly and putting them back in the drying cupboard?'

'Do you think they will dry?'

John nods. Mum and Dad aren't around. If we are quick we might get away with it. We go as fast as we can, squeezing as much water as we can into the bath. Then we spread them on the floor, fold them up neatly and put them in the cupboard. They look good. They are neatly folded and the floor is dry, which adds up to a good effort. John and I tiptoe off to our beds to sleep.

chapter twenty-three

Not everyone was asleep that night. Mick Mahon was awake, standing looking out his window, down on the yard at Wellington Central police station. A man was being taken out of a van and led into the receiving room where he would be fingerprinted, searched and put in a cell for the night. Later Mahon would wander down and find out what the charges were. In the meantime, he had more important things to be worrying about.

Murray McCarthy was sitting in the chair Jerry O'Connell had occupied earlier in the day. — No drink? McCarthy smiled up at Mahon.

— No.

McCarthy was surprised. Mahon had always been good for a drink.

— You want to know why I am not going to offer you a drink?

— It's not a problem, Mick. Not a problem. McCarthy was all confident arrogance.

— Don't Mick me.

— Not in a good mood?

— Never mind that. What about you? Where's the arrest? You have the bloody lot: body, means of transport and a motive. Frank was buggering around by not paying his debts, and that was pissing everyone off. They bloody smacked him with a spanner, put five bloody bullets in him and turfed him into Evans Bay. Christ, we even know where it happened. There's as much blood and hair flying around up there as on my wedding night.

— We're trying.

— Fuckin' bullshit!

— Hey. I've personally beaten the shit out of half the bookies in Wellington, and got fuck-all.

— Get *something*. Don't plant it. Don't fake it. Don't beat it out of anyone, but get something.

—All right, all right.

McCarthy looked hard at Mahon, a half-sneer across his mouth. — I suppose we're looking for a Protestant.

— I don't give a shit. If it's a Tyke then he drops for it. I want results.

— Look, I'm trying. McCarthy had been working for thirteen hours and he was getting tired.

Mahon put his face close to McCarthy's. The inspector's tobacco breath and a hint of the boiled cabbage he had eaten for dinner wafted over him. — There's trouble in this, Murray, and it's going to be on you.

McCarthy opened his mouth to protest. Mahon was snarling at him. — You bloody shut up and listen. It's over. There's a bloody lot changing, and it's leaving you behind. If you don't understand that then try this. There's this bloody great animal crashing around this place, looking for food. You'll do nicely. There's lots who'll put you on a plate, too.

McCarthy's mouth was open. He couldn't think of anything to say.

Mahon carried on. — You know what else is going on? There's trouble in bloody Miramar of all places. No one's been awake out there for years, and now they're talking about coppers being in with the slygrogs and loans. Who are they talking about, Murray? Eh?

— Jees, Mick, give it a rest.

— No. I've had enough. You've been in with the bookies for years and I've had enough.

McCarthy's eyebrows flew up and he began to push himself out of his seat. Mahon put a hand on his chest and pushed him back. — It's all right. You aren't the only one.

He took a breath. — What about this girl missing from Mount Vic? You know anything about that?

— No.

— You been up there and had a look?

— Course.

Mahon's face was only two inches from McCarthy's.

— And you never found anything?

— No. Will you stop it?

— I'll do whatever I like. You've lost your glow. Too many balls-ups. What about that queer in the chocolate factory in College Street? Another body lying around and no arrest. Unsolved!

McCarthy sensibly decided to say nothing.

—Frank's getting topped is just too much. People are scared where it'll lead. They're looking for safe, warm places. There's people going to be dobbed in and do a spell, even though they didn't do anything. It's going to take a lot of managing if it isn't going to do us all in. And you're going to be the first to go.

— I never took anything.

—Don't bloody lie! Mahon whipped his hand across McCarthy's face. — We need results, Murray. You need results. We want someone for Frank and we want that girl found, and if those two are connected up somehow, I'd better know first.

McCarthy checked his nose. No blood. He licked across his mouth. No blood there either.

— Well, piss off and get on with it, bloody quick.

Mahon stood back to let McCarthy stand up and looked at him. — You could end in the Mount if you're not careful. They're starting to line up to send you away. How long would you last? There's a few who'd come after the family while you were locked up.

— Is that a threat?

— Of course it's not a bloody threat! It's a guarantee. It's bloody closer than you think, too. You haven't got too many friends.

— What about you? Where are you, Mick? McCarthy looked frightened

— Nothing I can do. You've been running your own show too long. If you get this cleared up you might just get away with being allowed to retire and get out.

— Retire! I've got years before I retire.

— No, Murray. You're fucked. Come up with a winner for Frank, or it's the mincer for you.

Mahon was grinning at him. Murray McCarthy was not used to this, being sneered at. He felt slightly faint with the shock. He was nothing. All those years of striding around Wellington, the keeper of the Homo Register. He could ruin people's lives. It made him feel like God. And now he was next to finished. End up in Mount Crawford!

Mahon was flicking his hand, as if he was getting rid of an insect from his presence. McCarthy turned to the door, opened it and walked out. He was not going to close it. Mahon could do that. As he turned to the stairs, he heard the door close. Mahon had ambled over and kicked it shut, with no more thought for the door than he, or anyone else in this place, seemed to give for Murray McCarthy.

Out in Waring Taylor Street McCarthy stood still, trying to get control. Finally he took a deep breath and walked up to Lambton Quay. If he kept walking it would take him about twenty minutes to get to

Courtenay Place, and another five to walk up to above Oriental Bay, on Mount Victoria. If he was lucky a tram might take him part of the way.

No trams came, no matter how often he looked back and swore at the tram tracks. It took him slightly longer than twenty minutes to get to Courtenay Place. Marjoribanks Street was opposite. He would be climbing it, up to Hawker Street and starting from there. If he was going to go, then he was not going quietly.

chapter twenty-four

John and I tiptoe quietly towards the bush above Miramar North School. This is our chance to find out what is happening at their soccer practices. We have been allowed out of school early — there is supposed to be a First Communion practice but Father Bannon must have forgotten about it because he hasn't turned up. After about a half hour of waiting at the church we are all herded back to school, where they let us go a little bit early. John and I catch the tram up to Miramar North. We get off at Darlington Road and circle around.

Jane told us when they will be having their practice. To get this information she had to swap her third-favourite doll for Terry Taylor's sister's fourth-favourite one. Jane now has a big Negro mammy doll. You can take its clothes on and off, not like golliwogs which have the clothes all stitched on. The only good thing about golliwogs is that they are better for having on your pillow, because they are small and soft.

We are going through the Miramar transit camp, where the English and the Dutch people stay when they first come to New Zealand. We've never had much to do with them — they talk funny and always seem a bit confused about everything, and they all have trouble getting a proper suntan.

John and I creep along to the end of the transit camp, in case anyone from Miramar North School is keeping a lookout for spies. Eventually we find a place, behind some bushes, where we can see the Miramar North football field. Next to it are the two netball courts, and beside that the little building where Father Bannon, sometimes Father Reilly, says Mass for the Miramar North parishioners.

John spots the Miramar North team first. 'See, look! Can you see what they are doing?'

'There's nothing. All they are doing is practising passing, from the forwards back to the halves and then the backs.'

'Maybe they are going to do that, pass it back all the time?'

John wrinkled his nose. 'Nah, cause then they'd be going the wrong way all the time.'

I have to agree with that. John is good at spotting soccer stuff. That is probably why he has been in the Wellington reps three times, while I have only got in once.

'See, then they are passing it from the fullback out to the winger. The forwards are running at the goal and the winger is crossing it in front of them!'

This is definitely new. Most of the teams in our grade are happy to kick it up the middle. Then the forwards, and everyone else, chase after it. This is different. This looks like a really cunning tactic. No wonder Terry Taylor is so smug, when he isn't beating the life out of us.

We sit there for ages, nearly twenty minutes. The Miramar North team keep doing the same thing over and over again. Kick it back to the fullback, who kicks it out to Terry on the wing. The forwards rush, three at a time, at the goalkeeper. Terry crosses it and they kick it at the goal.

They look good. No, they look better than that. They look scary. We'll have to come up with something pretty good if we are going to beat them. The next thing is to see if they have a second plan.

No. They just keep doing the same thing; pass back to the fullback, then the winger, who crosses it for the forwards to score a goal. Up and down the field over and over again. It is always the same.

Maybe we have a chance if our forwards sprint as fast as they can and stop the ball getting out to their winger. Plus, that would leave us with the ball in their half of the field. It ought to be easy to get a goal from there. John is the important player. He is the fastest runner in our team, and he would get to their full-backs first.

There is a noise from further along in the bushes. John and I both put our hands up to signal we should be quiet. We smile at that, because we have had the same thought at the same time. I can't remember hearing a noise quite like it. It doesn't sound like a dog or a possum or any other sort of animal. We slither along on our stomachs, like we'd seen the soldiers doing in the war movies at the Saturday afternoon matinees.

It is one of the English people. He can't see us, but we can see he has his pants down. His bum is pure white and it has big red freckle-spots on it. He is lying on top of someone else. We can see it's a girl, because the person underneath has long hair and is sort of squealing in a voice that's higher than his.

He is sort of talking, in a gaspy voice, 'Fook, fook, fook. Bloody great, the old slippery, isn't it!' His bum is going up and down.

She lifts up one of her knees, so the sole of her foot is on the ground. She says 'Oh yes, Roger. Oh yes.'

I don't know, and I am too scared to ask John in case they hear us. It sounds to me as if he is getting more excited or desperate or something. She is breathing sort of funny too. We lie down as low as we can and watch. He is bigger than us, and if we try getting away he might hear us and chase us and beat us up.

'Could you take a bit more of the weight on your elbows, Roger,' she says.

'Sorry.' Then he goes back to, 'Fookin' 'ell, bloody fookin' 'ell.' Then he yells out, 'Look out, bugger's coming up pipe.' His bum goes faster and faster. He yells out 'Ooooh fookin' Mary.'

She says, 'My name is Jenny!' She says it as if she is a bit annoyed.

He flops down on her. 'I meant Mary, like in Jesus Christ! Sorry, did that spoil it? Hang on, let's have a look at you. No, it's all right. Spunk's all over place. Tons of it, lass, look. I did well here. There won't be any little tadpoles makin' way oop inside yer.'

'Can't you wait for a minute, Roger? We've just made love.'

John and I look at each other. Until now, we've thought 'making love' was kissing. We haven't seen these two doing any kissing.

'Do you mind rolling off, if you're finished that is. You're right on my bladder.'

'Oh sorry. There you go.'

'Thanks. It's just that I never went for a pee first.'

'Fookin' hell!'

'What's the matter? Do you want another one?'

'It's just the thought of all that fookin' romance in the air.' He copies her voice. 'Never went for a pee.'

'I can't help it.'

'Sorry, Jen. Lewk, it's just that now and again, and this isn't a complaint, because I really like the old slippery, it's just that sometimes you provide a wee bit mooch detail, if you know wha I mean.'

She doesn't look too pleased. She shakes her hair and pops her chest back into her dress. She stands up and pulls her underpants up and pulls her dress down over them. She is in a Saint Mary's College uniform.

He reaches up and holds the hem of her dress. 'Don't get angry, love. It's joost that I'm always hearing that sort of talk from missus over there in bloody Camp Kiwi.'

She frowns down at him.

'And wi' someone as beautiful as you it's a shame.'

She isn't quite as angry-looking now. 'That's better, Roger, because there's plenty of boys who want to do the same. I can get as much as I want!'

'Of course you can darlin'. It's just that I get a bit emotional, wi' lovemaking and all.'

She sits down beside him.

'That's a nice thing to say.'

She reaches over to his chin, and pulls his head around and kisses him. She drops her other hand down and puts it on the front of his pants. John and I look at each other. Maybe she is going to help him have a pee too!

He takes his mouth away. 'Bloody 'ell. You'd better stop that or there'll be another lot of slippery startin', and I better be off home.'

She takes her hand back, and they stand up.

'Next week?'

'It'll be all right next week,' she says.

'Eh, is it period?'

John and I know what periods are. When you go to secondary school you have different teachers instead of just one, like at primary school, and they teach you for a period, then you go off to another classroom.

'No, silly. Next week's my birthday. I'll be sixteen. I'll be legal.'

'Sixteen! Bloody 'ell. You never said you were under-age!'

'Well, it's all right now.'

'Bloody 'ell.'

'Stop saying bloody 'ell and give me a kiss, you silly man.'

'Silly's right. I don't think I could get a silly on after you tellin' me that. Gowd. Hope missus don't want shaggin' tonight.'

They give each other a quick kiss. 'Bye.' She grabs her school bag and is gone, off through the bush back towards Miramar.

The man is left standing there. 'Fookin' 'ell. Shaggin' bloody carnie. Can't believe it. I must be out of me fookin' mind.'

He turns around really quickly and starts walking straight at us. He is still doing up the buttons on his trousers when he sees us. John and I are too scared to move. 'How long 'ave you bin there?' he says.

We are too scared to say anything.

He shakes his head. 'Fookin' 'ell. I've bin shaggin a carnie and there's bin a couple of little Catholic buggers wi' little caps and ties peerin' oop me arse while I'm on nest. Fookin' 'ell. They won't believe this back in fooking Warrington. Oh well,' he says as he walks past us, 'it's back to concentration camp, wife, bloody kids, meat and two veg. Fookin' 'ell.'

He crashes off towards the transit camp. He obviously doesn't care whether anyone down on the Miramar North School field can hear him. John and I just sigh with relief because he didn't beat us up.

By the time we look back at the field, the football is finished. The Miramar North team is walking off the field. Still, there's one good thing. We know their secret plan.

We sneak around Miramar North School, going really fast through the transit camp in case we meet up with the man from Warrington. He might be in a better mood but we don't want to take a chance.

We go round Weka Street, to Camperdown Road, to go up to Totara Road and home up to Nevay Road. At the shops we see Jenny. She's got her bag over her shoulder and she's laughing and talking to a couple of boys from St Patrick's College. She is smiling up at the other boy, one of them, saying, 'But you are really good-looking. I bet you get all the girls to do anything you want!'

'What about you?' he says.

She laughs, waving her head around so her hair goes everywhere. 'I'm not interested in girls!'

He has a big stupid-looking smile all over his face. It keeps him distracted, long enough for us to get past and on the way up the hill.

When we get close to home we see Terry Taylor in the distance. He sees us too and gives us the fingers. He looks really angry. I wonder whether one of the adults has seen him hitting us and told our mum. I bet she rang up Mrs Taylor and Terry got into trouble.

That would be even more trouble for us.

When we get to our house our mum and dad are still talking about Dad's new job. 'It's a good job, and we don't know where it'll end,' he is saying.

'I've got a pretty good idea,' she says. 'You drink enough now.'

'I keep the family going and I never miss a day at work.'

'All right, all right,' she sighs and goes off into the kitchen.

Dad rubs his hand on the top of my head. 'One day, you'll be married, son.'

He doesn't look all that happy. I don't know what to say, so I don't say anything. That is the safest thing with adults. It is also a very bad idea in our house, where you have to speak up if you want to get noticed.

It is all very confusing.

chapter twenty-five

Father Reilly filled a kettle with water, lit a gas burner and put the kettle over it. The atmosphere between the priests had been frosty since he'd let loose with his sermon and that poor man had his head smacked in. Father Bannon and himself had been marched into the city. A Monsignor had given them the almighty of a shellacking. Father Bannon had got the worst of it, when he'd tried to shift the blame to Father Reilly.

Since then the atmosphere here had been appalling. Father Bannon seemed determined to stay in a bad mood. Father Reilly was getting tired of it. He had tried dropping hints about the ability of Jesus Christ to forgive those who had wronged him. The hint missed the mark.

He'd tried leaving a library book called *Coping in a Complicated World* lying around for Father Bannon to find. The parish priest said nothing. Instead, he flicked the book out the window. Father Reilly was left to sneak out in the middle of the night, to ferret through the dinner leftovers which Father Bannon dumped on top of the book.

Next day he took the book back to the library. He had to remind himself of Christ's stoicism in his sufferings on the Cross. The old bitch of a librarian started sniffing the book and began making loud remarks about priests deciding to use library books as ingredients for their onion soup. Actually it was the remains of a beef stew that had been dropped over the book, but he doubted that correcting the woman would turn things his way. Instead he mustered his dignity and strode out. Unfortunately he left his library card behind, and had to go and ask for it back, another win for the librarian.

This was still nothing beside the problem of Father Bannon and his angry silence. Surely the man was going to get over it. All priests had been disciplined, almost since their first day at the seminary. It was part of the making of a priest, putting strong personalities in front of him and making him obedient. In turn, if he was obedient enough, he would become the strong personality. It was the way of the Church, based on the benefits of thousands of years of dealing with seminarians.

However, it was obvious that Father Bannon was not going to get over it quickly. If anything, he seemed more determined than ever to hold on to his rage. Someone was going to have to pay for his humiliation, and that someone was going to be Father Reilly. If a book on coping was not going to work, then he would have to try something else. It would need to be a significant jump. A book on *Getting a Good Night's Sleep* was unlikely to fare any better. It was time for something more serious. Perhaps the answer lay in the dark side of the human condition. Specifically, sex.

This was too big a job for the little library in Chelsea Street. He changed into street clothes and caught the tram into the city. The librarian looked at him sideways when he asked if she had any books on the sin of Onan. We have Amman, which is a city near Egypt somewhere, and there's annals, which is about time, and there's . . .

— No. I want books on onanism. Self-abuse. The solitary sin.

— Just a minute. I'll see if I can help.

She was back in a couple of minutes, with three stern-looking women, all much older than him. The way they looked at him made him nervous. He repeated his request. — Onanism. Self-abuse. Books on it.

One of the women looked straight at him. — Most men come in looking for copies of *Ulysses* so they can

read Molly's soliloquy. Or *National Geographic* maga-
zines. We've got some books on childbirth, if that will
help. They've got pictures of people with no clothes on.

— No! he yelped. Her earnest seriousness was close
to destroying him. — I want theoretical information,
as to why people do it.

None of the women looked convinced, but
eventually the young woman librarian came back with
five books under her arm. — Here we are, she said as
she put them down on the counter. — *The Effects of
Masturbation, Masturbation: the links between self-abuse
and crime, Confessions of the Single Sinner, The male
continuum, Sex and Isolation* and *Studies of Sexual
Behaviour in Non-Integrated Communities.* — I hope there
is something there that will help.

Father Reilly blushed red with shame.

— Do you have your library card?

He handed it over.

— Thank you. She looked at it, holding it up between
her thumb and forefinger, surprised at the name. —
Father Reilly, she said, slightly emphasising the
'Father'.

Father Reilly grabbed his books and his library card
and ran from the library.

That night he left a book in Father Bannon's
bedroom, one in his study, another in the living room
and saved the other two for a second attack.

Next morning the two priests were eating their
Weet-Bix. Father Bannon was looking at him with an
intense gaze which Father Reilly was beginning to
find disturbing. This did not look like a man who

had spent the night quietly flogging himself into a peaceful sleep.

Father Bannon spoke. — Is there anything I should know, Father?

— Eh?

— The house is full of books on masturbation. I know you humiliated yourself with that sermon, but there is no need to succumb to the shallowness of transitory pleasure. Disgusting!

— I'm not . . .

— I see.

— You don't see.

— I am leaving. I have work to do. I'd suggest you keep away from the good, normal people of Miramar until you have learned better.

— But . . .

Father Bannon had stood up and was off. He turned at the door. — You could do worse than be thinking about repenting and how you can make yourself something more than a shallow apology for a priest.

Father Reilly was left gloomily contemplating his Weet-Bix. This had not gone well. He had arrived at Dante's Nineth Circle of Hell, where people could expect to suffer terribly for the rest of their lives. There was not much ahead except praying. Rosary after rosary. Eventually something would occur to him, a way to lift himself from this exquisite suffering. His life was in ruins, unless he could find a way to make a positive light shine down on him again.

chapter twenty-six

Dad has gone very quiet. His humour has disappeared, which is annoying Mum, because that's the reason she liked him in the first place. He's too unhappy even to play soccer, which is a shame because even though he isn't very good he makes sure Tony gets lots of kicks. That stops Tony grizzling, and we don't have to worry about Commissions of Inquiry descending on us.

Dad is quite old compared to a lot of the other fathers

at our school. He was thirty-five when the babies started arriving. Almost everyone else is in the mid to late twenties. It got a bit embarrassing at the Marist sports day. Dad was in the fathers' race and he was plugging along alone at the back of the field, but someone fell over so he didn't actually finish last.

He is quiet now because he and Mum are still sorting out this auditing job, and then there had been the Redemptorist priest talking about Dad getting into Parliament.

Mum is saying, 'But there is nothing to do at night except sit in the bar drinking. It's a waste of money. If we aren't going to move anywhere else we have to make the best of Miramar, and it's a pretty horrible place.'

Dad bridles at that. 'This is a very good house. Look at the view — you won't get that in too many places in the world. This is a great house.'

'It's just that we are all stuck up here, and you're off on some base where they don't have anything to do except sit around all night and drink.'

'It isn't like that,' he says but he doesn't sound too convincing, even to a little kid like me.

'No?'

'No!'

There is a long silence. Mum sighs. So does Dad. Then there is more silence.

'Is it possible you won't spend the evenings drinking?'

'I don't drink that much.'

'Huh!'

The discussion goes round and round like that.

Nothing much is changing. Dad is going to end up with the job: he will be in Wellington for a week, then away for a week, then back for two. And then it starts again.

Every time he goes away, he makes the same little speech. He leans down and says to me, 'I am going to be away for a few days. You are the oldest. You have to help your mother, and be the man.'

I am eight and a half. I don't know how to be the man and I don't want to be one, except when there is something exciting going on. If the exciting stuff goes wrong, or it turns into a mess I don't want to be a man. I want someone to snuggle me up and read to me.

I like getting read to. The older kids at school have stopped that, and say it's kid's stuff. They've told me that if I stop getting read to and concentrate on sport, they will let me play with them. So I stopped Mum reading to me, and I was hurt when the big kids didn't seem to take any notice. They just said stuff like, 'You're too little and you couldn't keep up with us, so you aren't playing. Go away!'

That decision is always final. So I've ended up with no sports with the big kids, and I don't get any stories read to me either. It is very confusing, this business of being a man.

It is also a bit less happy at our place when Dad is away. Sometimes it gets worse when he comes back. That's because he has been this presence in the background. When Mum is over-stressed and tired and having trouble coping with all the kids, he becomes a threat: 'Your father will talk to you about this when he gets back.' That makes us a bit nervous, because he's this slightly scary figure hovering over us, who will swoop down, with lightning bolts and thunderclaps going off all round him, and who could do terrible things, like cutting off the ice cream and opportunities to watch senior soccer games.

Then, when he does arrive home, he is usually exhausted and all he wants to do is cuddle the kids and enjoy the buzz and energy. He doesn't want to start working through a list of crimes and begin announcing sentences.

Mum knows this and sometimes the charges get dropped before they get to court, in case she ends up getting a list of 'case dismissed' which weakens her position for investigating and restoring order at future crime scenes.

Only Dad is still tired, and he sometimes has a few beers to take the edge off the travelling and concentration of the week. It makes him a bit distant, because he sometimes just wants to retreat into peace and quiet, which is annoying for both us and Mum because after two weeks together we have all started to get on each other's nerves.

Brother Brian has decided to have parent/teacher nights. He invites all the parents down to the school so the Marist Brothers can tell them what is happening with their kids. The parents all think that is a terrific idea. The pupils, all except the swots and the brainboxes and the ones who never get into trouble, which means the ones who never do anything at all, think it is a terrible idea.

One of the parent/teacher nights is on when Dad is down at the Wigram Air Force Base, just outside Christchurch. Mum is trying hard to get there. She gets one of the women from along the road to babysit us. Babysitting! She includes me in that. What happened to being the man?

At 6.30, the babysitter has an emergency of some sort. It's too late to find anyone else. Mum, who is desperate to get down to the school to find out about her boys, and to get down off the Nevay Road hill and have an hour or so with the other parents, is stuck at home. That isn't helping with the atmosphere over Dad's job.

Then, just after that, John and I get into a huge fight with some kids from Worser Bay School. There are five of them against the two of us. Even though we've done boxing, we end up losing. One of them steals John's cap. I think it's thrown away because even though the teacher at Worser Bay tries to find it, he doesn't have any luck. We end up having to buy a new cap.

Apparently there would be a better chance of finding the cap if Dad were home. He says that the teacher who looked for the cap isn't very interested in anything women say or do, so if a father had asked him to find John's cap he would have made more of an effort. I think Mum knows that, and it doesn't help.

There are lots of things like that which makes Dad's job, even though he is getting more money than a lot of our neighbours, not very popular in our house.

chapter twenty-seven

Friday night was normally the night when Dad had a few beers, if there wasn't a rapid raffle going on. There was one Friday night he wasn't drinking much. Pat Conlin had turned up, looking tired and unhappy. He had been at Wellington Central police station and wanted to be around some friendly faces.

He came in our back door and sort of flopped down at our dining-room table. 'The bloody coppers have been beating the crap out of me, Kev.'

'For that Frank bloke they pulled out of Evans Bay?'

'They belted me around every way they knew, and after all I have done for those bastards!'

Dad looked at him. I was hiding in a corner and I could see Dad was worried. 'You aren't going to do anything silly, are you?' he asked.

'I'm too old for rough stuff with coppers now, Kev. Besides the government's bringing in an off-course tote. No one'll bother with bookies then.'

Mum wasn't sitting around. She'd often told Dad she thought Pat was nothing but a crook. Dad had said he liked it when Pat turned up. It was a look at another world, all dark and dangerous, and he didn't have to worry about anything horrible happening to him.

'There's that girl missing too.'

Dad stopped looking keen and interested at this. I didn't know why. Later he said it was because his kids were starting to grow up, and the idea of a teenager disappearing was getting too close to home.

'She's not mixed up in it personally, but there's people around her who are part of it all. The coppers haven't got on to that yet.'

'Jesus, Pat. There are some things I just don't want to know.'

Pat wasn't taking much notice. 'I'm going to get the bastards back, Kev. They stuck me face up against a wall and smacked me in the kidneys. They put me in a chair and clouted me round the head with telephone books. There isn't a mark on me, but shit I'm hurt.'

'I don't think I can help with it, Pat.'

I liked that, Dad not wanting to be part of something happening outside our family.

Pat stood up. 'I just came to see you before I left. Like I said, Kev, it's over.'

'Where are you going?'

Uncle Pat looked at him as if he had done something horribly wrong. He didn't say anything. Dad nodded. Pat didn't want to say, at least not right then. He was talking to the right person, though. Dad knew a little bit about getting out of a country. Before I was born he worked as a radio operator on ships. He'd got a job on a ship which was supposed to be going to Hong Kong and then all round the world. It paid big money. Only he thought it was American dollars and the shipowners thought it was Hong Kong dollars, which were worth a lot less. He jumped ship when it got to Melbourne and came back to Wellington.

I was really impressed with this, because I thought he had climbed over the side and jumped, and swum into Australia. I was a bit disappointed when Dad laughed and said there were ways you could get into a country by dodging the Customs and hiding out. He got slipped onto a ship going back to Wellington — they called it 'travelling ringbolt'. He never told me what that meant. But if he had not done that I might never have been born.

Uncle Pat stood up. He ruffled my hair but didn't say anything. He looked round for Mum to say goodbye. Dad called out to her. 'Pat is leaving now!'

She came out and stood between the kitchen and the living room, still holding her teatowel. She and Uncle

Pat looked at each other. I think he realised she didn't like him very much. He smiled a little smile. She smiled back, but she wasn't very enthusiastic. He shook hands with Dad again, and ruffled my hair again. He turned around and walked out very quickly. I stood at the window and watched him going down the path, to his big black car parked down on Nevay Road.

Dad turned to Mum. 'Well, that's the end of an era, and we won't see any more like him.'

'Of course we will,' she snorted. 'If there's easy money there's always more like him.'

'He's a relative!' Dad was trying to say.

'I don't care.'

Dad looked out the window, down to where Pat's car had been parked. He didn't say anything. I didn't know what he was thinking. Maybe he was thinking that Pat lived an exciting life, doing whatever he wanted, whenever he liked, and getting a huge amount of money. Then he sighed and got busy with helping get the kids to bed.

Maybe he'd decided that what he had might not have been so terrible, because he wasn't nearly sixty and having to smuggle himself on ships and sneak out of the country in the middle of the night. He had a bit of a look in his eye which we had seen before. John and I hopped into our beds without making a fuss, in case we got him angry and he started snapping at us.

I had to go out to the toilet, because I had been in such a hurry when I thought Dad was going to get annoyed. I snuck into the bathroom. When I came out I saw Dad sitting there at the kitchen table. Mum had gone off to bed because she was tired. He was looking away into the distance, not even taking any notice of the glass of beer he had sitting there in front of him. He looked sad.

chapter twenty-eight

Mum seems to have given up trying to talk Dad into looking for another job, one where he comes home every night instead of going all round the country. He seems to be much happier now he is able to get away for about a week a month. Over the first month there were lots of conversations between them, which always seemed to go along the same track:

'When are you going away again?'

'Next week.'

'When will you be back?'

'Probably Friday afternoon. I'll go into the office and I'll be home at about half-past five or a quarter to six.'

'How much time will you be spending in the bar when you are away?'

'Not long. Look, there's nothing much else to do when you are stuck out there in the country.'

'You could read a book.'

'I don't read books.'

'Oh.'

'Oh hell, what does that mean?' he would say, sounding exasperated.

'I just don't think it's a very good idea for you to be in the bar every night, that's all.'

'I'm not an alcoholic or anything. I can manage. I don't embarrass anyone.'

'All right. If that's what you think.'

Then there was a long silence. Normally that was when they started looking around, and they'd see me. If it was daytime I was chased out to play. If it was raining I'd have to go up to the other end of the house and read a book. If it was night, I'd have to go off to bed. The only place I didn't stay was right there.

I sometimes think I would like it better if there wasn't any beer in the world, because then everyone would be happy.

No they wouldn't.

Terry Taylor and James Wilson don't drink beer, and they are always causing trouble. I think that's because their fathers don't like Catholics very much. Terry Taylor's father tried for years to get in the Wellington rugby team, but a Marist prop always got picked ahead of him. If he couldn't get into the Wellington team, it meant he was never going to achieve his dream of being an All Black.

James Wilson's father decided he didn't like Catholics after he caught his wife having an affair with a man called Dermott Mulcahay. I don't know what an affair is, but no one ended up happy. We can tell, because James Wilson changed. Since then the only time he doesn't poke fun at Catholics is when he plays in our street games.

Everyone else seems to be always drinking beer. They drink a lot of it at the parish balls. They aren't balls at all. That's too elegant. They are more like local hops, but the organisers call them balls, probably because they have bands, which are never very good. Most of the bands have a man on the saxophone, another one on the piano, a drummer and maybe a guitar player. They would get on stage and keep churning out the songs till half-past midnight. The mums would try and get the dads to have a few dances before the dads got too drunk to push around the dance floor.

It used to be even more complicated because the dances were held in the Rio Grande hall, next door to the church. It was on the first floor, up a steep wooden staircase. A lot of people had got full of beer and fallen down the stairs. Fortunately no one was killed. Dad had an explanation for this: 'It's all right if you fall down when you're drunk, because you're relaxed and that means you don't get hurt.'

I'm not sure about this theory. Veronica, a girl at Holy

Cross, had her dad fall down some stairs at home. He was in hospital for a year. When he came out, he couldn't keep a job and he used to go around yelling at people. One day he went into his garden shed with his shotgun. Jerry O'Connell and some other policemen had to spend all day persuading him to come out. They took him back to hospital after that.

Some of the older boys teased Veronica about her father being in the loony bin. Eventually, about six months later, Veronica and her mother moved to Auckland.

Mum and Dad had missed the first few parish balls because Dad didn't like dancing. Mum was a bit disappointed about that. But it all changed when Dad heard about all the beer they had there. The ballet and ballroom dancing teachers, who shared the Rio Grande, used to get hacked off about this because they would spend the year getting the floor all slippery and perfect for dancing. The day after the parish ball the floor was a bit less slippery after pavlova, sausage rolls, tomato sauce, fish sandwiches and beer had all been mashed into it. It was a smelly mix and it was usually enough to stop the dancers in their tracks.

This was something else that ended up with Father Bannon. Every year the ballroom dancing teachers, a husband and wife, would arrive at Father Bannon's door. — What are you going to do about it? they would demand.

— What?

— Drunken Catholics dropping rubbish on our floor. The place reeks of beer.

Every year Father Bannon would bristle. — I hope it won't twist the lives of your pupils forever more.

They didn't like the parish ball, ever since the previous year when they were invited to do a demonstration of ballroom dancing at the Rio Grande. The Marist Rugby Club had taken a lot of tickets and were getting a bit drunk by the time the demonstration came along. The footballers struggled to see the art and grace in ballroom dancing, although they liked the idea of getting a woman to put her stomach right against theirs. Otherwise, they dismissed it as being for 'poofters'. They yelled this, loudly.

The ballroom-dancing husband had been a Commando during World War II, working in the jungles ahead of the army. He stopped the exhibition, walked over to the bloke who was making the most noise and belted him on the nose. Then he dropped into a karate stance, which suggested that he knew what he was doing. The rest of the team thought this over, and decided the safest thing was to redirect their jeering towards their teammate.

— Who's the poofter now! They laughed at him.

— Never mind that shit. I'm gonna do 'im.

The Marist coach grabbed him and sat him down. — No you're not. There's the big game with Poneke next week, and you've gotta be right.

The coach had a bright idea. He waved to the injured player's girlfriend. — Look, what's yer name.

Mary.

— Jim is a bit knocked about. He's embarrassed and humiliated. His spirit needs a bit of restoring. I don't suppose you could whip 'im home and, you know, give 'im a bit of help with that which no man can provide.

Mary did not look pleased. — No. I'm not doing that. I'm not a slut. I'm not doing that till I get married.

The coach muttered. — Listen to ya. Bloody whinin' moll. You're no use if ya won't do ya bit for the team!

Mary looked across at the dancing teacher. This gave her an idea. She swung a passable right cross at the coach, and connected with his left cheekbone. He staggered back. Two of his team had to make a quick decision. They knew that Mary was being economical with the truth when she said she was saving herself for marriage, but finally decided this might not be the best moment to start a discussion about it.

Mary marched out and down the Rio Grande's stairs. By then the dancing teacher was out on the footpath. His wife had yelled at him for demeaning himself, and her, for getting involved in a street brawl and had driven off, leaving him to walk home.

Mary and the dancing teacher agreed they had both been magnificent. They hugged. He stroked her head and rubbed her shoulders. She said he was too good and too talented for places like this. She took his hand and they walked away from the Rio Grande. He offered her his handkerchief to wipe away the tears. They looked into each other's eyes, and spent the next hour and a half having vigorous sexual intercourse on the grass underneath the balcony of the Miramar Aces softball team's clubrooms at the Polo Ground.

Sadly, the dancing teacher's wife found out. This added fire to her efforts to have the parish ball banned.

Years later the dancing teacher told Dad, 'I never got any more sex, but then there was nothing new about that. I wasn't getting any at home anyway, not unless it was a bit of the old owner-operated.'

The wives had to listen to his wife wailing, 'I spend the year teaching people to waltz and foxtrot properly, and when they get the chance to do it they just sit around and drink beer, spill their food on the floor and talk about rugby.'

Dad chuckled when he heard about that. 'The men are pretty bad too,' he said, with a big smile on his face.

'You see.' Mum said later to Terry Taylor's mother, at our house to collect some clothes Jane had grown out of, 'that's why I married him. Just when you've had enough and you're going to run off, out comes that damn sense of humour, and you can forgive just about anything.'

Dad heard that, even though we were in the next room. He beamed a huge smile. 'Don't you worry, son. There's nothing to forgive.'

He was wrong. There was, because that was a Saturday and Jack turned up again, with his beer and he stayed and wanted to sing World War II songs. He was still there at nearly midnight, even though everyone was exhausted. — He was only interested in leaving when all his beer was finished. All the singing and stuff, and Mum having to come out to the dining room where they were sitting and beg Jack to go home, meant there was definitely going to be a bit to forgive.

Next day Dad spends almost all afternoon playing soccer with us, even though he really would have liked to spend it asleep, because of the beer. I guess it is a punishment of some sort.

He gets a bit better, though, when he kicks the ball over the garden. 'You kids stay there. I'll go and get it,' he yells out and takes off after the ball. He waves at us to stay where we are. So we wait.

Once he is out of sight, near the pine trees, we hear this funny sound. It is the noise people make when they are being sick. Vomiting. A couple of minutes after that, he comes back with the ball. He starts playing much better. He makes sure little Tony scores a couple of goals, and lets me and John have heaps of shots at the goal.

After about an hour we get a bit tired of soccer and the game winds up. John and I go down to look at where Dad had lost the ball. There is a big pool of sick drying there. We know it is his, because he's had the same lunch as us, with peas, carrots and potato. They are all lying there on the grass under the pine trees. He has been really, hugely sick.

John and I have a good look. There is one good thing — he hasn't sicked up any of the roast lamb. That is good, because the week before, when we had lost our pocket money somewhere, he told us how expensive everything was, and he had picked out the Sunday roast as an example of how much money it cost to keep our family going. He obviously meant what he said, because he hasn't vomited up any meat, at least there isn't any we can see. We wait, because the cat from next door comes sniffing at the sick, and I reckon that if there is any meat there the cat will find it, even if it means getting its paws all dirty.

I think Mum has seen all this happen, because when Dad kicked the ball away and chased it, she and Terry Taylor's mother were sitting at the window. They stopped sorting through the pile of clothes and looked out the window, with big smiles on their faces.

When she leaves to go home, I hear Terry Taylor's mother saying, 'I must get Jim out playing soccer. He's been putting on a bit of weight. Maybe he can eat the same, play a bit of soccer, and sick it up. Then I won't have to feed him as much. I might save a bit on the grocery bills.'

They both laugh.

I wonder whether Dad has heard this.

chapter twenty-nine

I also wonder whether Terry Taylor knows his mum is drinking tea with his enemy's mum. John and I are getting fed up with him, because he's gone back to being totally smug. We have to struggle not to let it slip that we know his team's plan, and now his mum is here so we have to keep quiet in front of her.

It is getting stressful and difficult.

When we get to school there is lots of talk about the

Miramar North game. Before school starts, no one in our class is talking about anything else. It is starting to look as if our soccer game is turning into a religious war.

Brother Virgilius, one of the old Marist Brothers, hears some of us talking about the game and how important it is to beat the Protestants. He chuckles, an odd sound coming from somewhere in his leathery old throat. 'You should have been here thirty years ago.'

That's over three times our whole lives! We wait very politely to see what he is going to say. 'Yes Brother,' we say, almost together.

He smiles at us. 'Not only would you not have been playing Miramar North, you would have been going home in groups to make sure you weren't attacked because you were Catholics.'

Get attacked! That all stopped when we learned boxing. Not too many people, except for Terry Taylor, are game to attack Catholics any more in case they get the Marist boys after them.

He is a bit old, so we keep quiet and let him talk. He goes on about ghettos and being outnumbered and having to be careful and everything. He has told us all this before. I think he is wrong. We only have to add up the numbers of Catholics versus everyone else on Nevay Road. We have heaps of people. We have nearly an army, if we can persuade all the mothers to let our soldiers out at the same time.

I can't think of as many Miramar North boys who live up around here. Most kids go to Worser Bay School and we don't have to worry about them too much, because we don't play any big soccer games against them.

Brother Virgilius obviously doesn't realise that up on Nevay Road there is a bit of doubt as to whether there is a Catholic ghetto. We think we might have the numbers. Instead, there would be a Protestant ghetto. Terry Taylor and James Wilson would be in it, especially Terry Taylor. If we are lucky it might end up with him being the only one.

That makes us the aces. We can start a religious persecution, like the ones we read about in the books, where the saints have to suffer horribly before they become saints. Only Protestants would be suffering, and that is even better, because they can't get made up into saints afterwards. Wow!

I ask John about this. 'If we were running the persecution, would that make us the bad guys?'

He frowns and thinks about it for a minute. 'Do we get to bash up Terry Taylor and James Wilson?' is his hesitant answer.

'Definitely!' I say, because I can sense this was going in the right direction.

'Yeah.' He has a big smile on his face. 'If we do the bashing up, that means we are in charge, so that means we aren't the bad guys.'

I'm not sure quite how that works.

He is, because one of the kids at school, whose father works in the Labour Party, told him: if you are in charge you can beat up anyone, and you get elected again.

I'm still not sure. He is right about the Labour Party people, though . . . They sometimes have meetings at our house, and talk a lot about what they will do when they make it back to being the government. The idea seems to be to do terrible things to the National Party people who are now doing terrible things to them. It is all a bit complicated for me.

When the Labour people talk about being in government, they are inclined to go a bit dreamy-looking, like the cowboys in the westerns at the Capitol when they look at their girlfriends and say there is a big world out there with plenty of room for everyone, as soon as they have killed all the Indians.

If the Labour and National Parties are out to get revenge on each other and the cowboys want to kill all the Indians, then it must be all right for me and John to start a religious persecution, especially against Terry Taylor and James Wilson.

John looks a bit dubious. 'Do you think it is a very good idea to tell Mum we are starting a religious persecution?' he says, in a slightly worried way. He has a point. He is looking over to where Mum is talking to Terry Taylor's mum. They are laughing.

John frowns. 'I bet if we said we were going to start a persecution, they would think it was funny.'

I bet the monks who ran the Spanish Inquisition never worried about the humiliation of being laughed at by their mothers. This is a thought which should be enough to stop me, but it doesn't. I like the idea of this persecution business.

Mum is walking back from saying goodbye to Terry Taylor's mother when I announce the news. 'We are going to start a Miramar Inquisition and the Catholics are going to run everything and the Protestants are in big, big trouble!'

'That's nice,' she says as she carries on up to the house, obviously thinking about other things. I hope one of them is our dinner.

Nice! Nice? What is that supposed to mean? What decent religious persecution ever prospered on 'nice'. I might not have reached ten but I know a few things. I know a persecution needs hate and fury, just like a good soccer game. Nice is useless.

Then she makes it worse. She gets to the back door and says to the leader of the Miramar Religious Persecution, 'Come and have your dinner, and don't forget it's your turn to wash the dishes, and then you have to do your homework.' Obviously it is not going to be easy to get this persecution boat out of the docks.

Anyway, I have to forget about it for a couple of days. The soccer season is hotting up. We have just played Miramar South at the Crawford Green field. We win 1–0, when Micky Marsline boots in a goal seconds before the referee blows the whistle for the finish.

There is a bit of a fuss about that. Their coach refereed the first half and our coach, Mr O'Malley, is in charge of the second half. Their coach is starting to make angry remarks about how long the second half is lasting, stuff like 'the Thousand Year Soccer Game', and how it is amazing the full-time whistle goes as soon as we score a goal.

Mr O'Malley looks at him and says in a very loud

voice, 'Remember, boys, it is just as important to be gracious winners as it is to be gracious losers.' He makes a point of saying the word 'losers' specially loud.

Their coach says something about 'smart tyke pricks'.

Then Mr O'Malley gets going on this really loud lecture, full of stuff about 'ignoring bigots and the narrow-minded' and how 'mature men know how to lose' and 'taking pity on people who do their best but aren't very good and get jealous of those with more talent'.

Just as he leads our team into the dressing room, and when he thinks we aren't watching, Mr O'Malley gives the Miramar South coach a big smile and then flicks the fingers sign at him.

The other coach strides over to Mr O'Malley's car, undoes the front of his pants and pees on the door. While he is holding his cock with one hand, he half-turns and gives the fingers back towards our dressing room.

Mr O'Malley walks over. 'Didn't I mention it? I borrowed the car off Jerry O'Connell, the policeman. He's very fussy about it.'

Their coach gets such a fright he loses his aim and his wee goes all over the front of his trousers. He has light grey pants and we can see the big wet patches.

By then almost all of us are out of the dressing room. Mr O'Malley points at their coach's pants and says in a loud voice, 'See, that's how half-arsed losers behave.'

The Miramar South coach looks as if he might throw

a punch at Mr O'Malley, but he probably decides that Mr O'Malley might be too big and strong for him, so he just lopes off across Crawford Green, giving the fingers as he goes.

He is halfway across when it starts raining. That's lucky, because the rain covers up the wee marks on his pants. He makes a run for his car, and only slips over once on the wet grass. He gets to the car and yells at the top of his voice that we are 'nothing but a cheating pack of little Tyke cunts'.

Mrs Costello, who has come along to see her Anthony playing fullback for our team, asks him exactly what he means, using that sort of language. He starts up his car and takes off incredibly fast. The back wheels are spinning and the back of his car is fishtailing up Broadway towards the Seatoun tunnel. He still has his hand out the driver's door, giving us the fingers.

When he has gone, Jimmy Hannam puts his hand up. Mr O'Malley nods. 'Excuse me, sir?' he said. 'What's a cunt?'

Mr O'Malley sort of splutters a bit. Mrs Costello has a big smile on her face. I think she knows, and wants to hear what Mr O'Malley will say. He looks as serious as he can.

'Um, um,' he says, 'it's what losers call you when you beat them 1–0, and you do it with a brilliant goal. Come on. Hurry up. We've got to go!' He starts waving us to the two cars the parents have brought to drive us back to school.

That's when we find out we have a new coach. Mr O'Malley says it has been wonderful fun and he couldn't think of going out on a higher note. But he has a new job and that is that.

Mrs Costello is saying that she is going to coach us. That will make her the only woman soccer coach in the Under-11 eastern suburbs league. No other schools know about this yet, because she won't be on the sidelines until next week, so it is all right. I guess we have about a week before we start getting laughed at because we haven't got a proper man for a coach.

There is one good thing about it — Mrs Costello brings lot of oranges. She says she will bring a double lot if we do just one thing. We get nervous. If we have to wear dresses, that's it. We are joining the rugby team.

But it is all right. The condition is that when we have the next game, we have to stand in our positions and pass the ball to each other. No one takes a shot at goal until there have been 10 passes, and no running in a pack. It sounds as though it will take the fun out of the game, which is making huge runs at the goal.

We have a practice against the Thirds. We get a huge surprise when her tactic works. So do the Thirds. They are running everywhere. They start to get a bit angry and things get a bit dirty, because they have to knock us over to get the ball.

Mrs Costello yells out, 'Good boys!'

When we forget, she puts her fingers in her mouth and whistles. It is terrific. There are seagulls sitting on the grass a hundred yards away, and as soon as she whistles they flap away into the sky.

Jimmy Hannam gets a goal, sticking out his foot when their centre-half tries to clear the ball. It bounces in for a 2–1 score. She lets out another whistle which stops everyone, and yells out, 'That's that. The game's over.'

Their coach runs up. 'There's still ten minutes to go.'

'Don't argue with me, Jack Halloran. The game's over.'

'Look, there's still time on the clock. What do you know about soccer?'

'About as much as you learn every night in Jim McClaverty's slygrog.'

He stops and doesn't say anything more. It is the end of the game.

We stand around her and watch him go. This is going well.

chapter thirty

Murray McCarthy stood in the rough, scrubby bush above Hawker Street near the corner with Marjoribanks Street and clenched his fist on his torch. Marie West's body was there at his feet. By the look of her she had been there for all the three months she had been reported as gone. The bastards had said they had searched the bush, all of it. They bloody hadn't. He had only been poking around up here for an hour and he'd found it. Unless someone had hid the body and dumped it up here after the police search was over.

Not that the girl was worried. Her body was half-covered with dust and dirt. One of her legs and an arm were sticking out at a funny angle. He could see only half her face. Her eye was open, staring out at a world she was never going to see again. This was always the way. The eyes! They always went flat and dull. It always made him feel uncomfortable.

God, she was only seventeen, just a kid.

He dared not risk moving the body. There would be photographers and experts crawling all over it soon enough and they would know if someone had moved anything in the last twenty-four hours. It was bad enough that he'd walked up this close. His footprints would be there.

Above him dark clouds were lining up to treat Wellington to a night of nature's theatre — wind, rain, possibly some lightning. Excellent. That'd get rid of the footprints.

He looked down at her and took off his hat. It was the least he could do, a bit of respect for her in this, her third-to-last resting place. Tomorrow she would be in the morgue being sliced up so the doctors could find out how she died. Then there would be a coffin and a funeral and either cremation or burial, probably up in the Karori cemetery.

He bent over her. There was string around her neck, knotted under her chin. That was different. Usually the knot was at the back, because the killer had attacked from behind. Not here. Whoever did this had looked her right in the eye as he choked the life out of her. The terror and fear as she'd looked up at him hadn't mattered. A bloody monster!

He stepped back. His shoulders dropped and he closed his eyes.

He had caused this.

Somehow, somewhere along the way, the Frank Wilkins murder was mixed up in this. She'd gone only about a week after him, and half the people around her were mixed up with the loan sharks and the bookies. The police suspected her father of being in with the bookies. He'd been in to Central and they'd hammered away at him for hours. All he'd admit was giving her a black eye, and that they'd had some serious arguments, but that was all. Now this.

She'd seen or heard something about someone who was scared enough to do this. They'd risked the drop for her, so it was serious.

If it was her father, what was the bastard like deep down? Who could hide his kid's body till the coppers had gone, then drag it up through the dark bush and cover it up so it wouldn't be found. Or just dump it there and hope the coppers wouldn't find it? McCarthy had always thought he was tough, hard and cold, but he was nothing compared with this.

He picked his way out to Marjoribanks Street. He was shaken. Murray McCarthy, the hounder of homosexuals, the man with his hand in the bookies' pockets, the man who knew the secrets, who inspired fear, was shaking in his shoes.

He remembered to turn his torch off, in case someone

saw him. He'd have to admit he was lucky. He had been prepared to spend all night up there, sweeping back and forwards as a one-man search party.

He snorted. — Lucky! Jesus.

He kept clenching and unclenching his fists as he walked down to Hawker Street. He stopped outside the West house, looking up at the soft yellow lights in the windows. He could see her parents' heads. They were drinking tea and listening to the radio, just like every other family in Wellington.

What was it like for the mother? McCarthy winced. She must have been blotting out the thought that her child was dead, hoping she had run off with a boy or gone somewhere to have a baby, or both. There would have been her prayers that one day there would be a knock on the door and she would be standing there, crying and looking for love.

If her husband had done it, she would know and be burying it as deep as she could, always knowing. If not, they were still left, not knowing.

McCarthy had heard the coppers down at Central drinking their tea while they took a break from grilling her father. It was always the same theme. When he breaks that's it. But they didn't break him. Perhaps he was innocent. Thoughts. Thoughts. Thoughts.

McCarthy thought about a man sitting up there eating his dinner and drinking his tea, letting his wife suffer the nights of not knowing, letting her hold on to her fragment of hope, knowing there was no hope, that his daughter was rotting in the bush less than a hundred yards away.

A man and a woman were walking up the road towards McCarthy. They looked nervous, worried about the man standing there, snorting his breathing and glaring up at the houses on the other side of the road. He shook his head and turned away down Hawker Street, not trusting himself to look back. If he did, he wasn't sure he wouldn't run up the stairs to the house and kick the girl's father until his eye stared up, dull and unseeing, like his daughter. An eye for an eye.

He had kicked and beaten people before, lots of them. This would be different, a long way past trying to get a confession. If he killed him he could end up in a cell himself, spending the night before they came to hang him. Thoughts.

As McCarthy walked down to Courtenay Place he slowly calmed down enough to think about the problems. Obviously, the first was the body. It had to be found, but not by him. If he marched into Central and announced it, there would be questions. The last person he wanted to face was Mick Mahon, especially after their last chat.

Besides, he needed the weather to get rid of his footprints.

McCarthy reached Courtenay Place and stood beside the Embassy Theatre. He looked around and saw a red Austin parked over near the Taj Mahal. That was the answer. Now he knew what to do. He shook his head as he crossed to the toilets. Didn't Freddy ever learn?

He stopped outside. A man was coming out of the building, glancing around to see if anyone had seen him. As soon as he spotted McCarthy his face went pale and he sprinted down to Wakefield Street and was gone.

'Lucky boy. Last night you'd have been fitted up and into the Register. Lucky, lucky, lucky.'

McCarthy was outside the entrance and closed his eyes. It was always darker in there than the outside, because the queers were always breaking the light bulbs to make it easier to escape if the police arrived. McCarthy also wanted to be ready for action. He had some hard experience of how well some of the homos could fight when they decided they weren't going quietly.

This time was all right. There was no one around. Only one cubicle door was closed, at the end and furthest from the entrance. McCarthy shook his head. Freddy, Freddy, Freddy. You've been told, not once but a dozen times—you meet them here and you take them somewhere else to bugger them. He took a breath and booted the cubicle door open.

A pair of buttocks was pistoning backwards and forwards. McCarthy smiled. Sure enough, it was Freddy. His trousers were around his ankles. In front of him was another man, standing on the toilet bowl and leaning back. To stop himself falling he held the overhead cistern with both hands.

Freddy looked over his shoulder. His mouth dropped open when he saw McCarthy. The policeman grabbed him by his jacket collar and yanked him back out of the cubicle. Without Freddy to keep him in place the other man fell back on the cubicle floor, trying to stand up and hoist his trousers at the same time.

McCarthy was careful not to be too violent with Freddy. The little man had been one of New Zealand's most promising boxing talents, seriously talked-about for a world title. McCarthy had first-hand experience. He had been too vigorous when arresting Freddy five years before. Freddy had slipped into boxing mode, ducked under McCarthy's punch and broken the policeman's jaw with a vicious little left rip. As McCarthy sagged, Freddy had whipped an uppercut through the policeman's non-existent defence, adding a broken nose for McCarthy to show the hospital doctors. Freddy got two years in Mount Crawford for that.

Times had changed. The two had come to an understanding, based on Freddy's willingness to help McCarthy out by beating up someone too powerful or too important for the police to be involved. In turn, Freddy was reasonably sure it would take being caught in the act of murder for McCarthy to arrest him. Otherwise he was safe.

The fat little man who had been obliging Freddy was hopping to the door, wrestling with his underpants and trousers and braces as he shuffled out the door, his face an alabaster white.

Freddy looked at him and smiled. — It's all right. He's not here to belt one into you!

The fat man's mouth dropped open as he fled.

— Freddy, I've got a job for you, McCarthy said.

— Oh no, not another try at stitching up a member of Parliament!

—Jesus, McCarthy snapped. — Will you bloody shut up! Someone might come in for a piss and hear you.

— We're even, Murray. I did the last job, that's it.

— For God's sake, Freddy! I just caught you pumping away at that joker's arse. That's good for two years up in the Mount!

— The evidence just walked away. Freddy pointed out.

— I don't give a bugger.

The two men stopped, smiling at the accidental pun. McCarthy continued. — This is different, Freddy, and I don't want a bloody song and dance about it, either.

— I am not killing anyone!

— No, the exact opposite. I want you to find someone. Tomorrow morning. It's that West sheila from Mount Victoria. She's in the bush up above Hawker Street, near Marjoribanks Street.

— Jesus Murray. Did you kill her?

— No, I bloody didn't! Just shut up and listen.

— Sorry. I'm a bit agitated. I get like that when I'm stopped in the middle of a good hard root and someone asks me to go and find sheilas that've been missing for months.

— Are you going to do it for me?

— What about getting my name out of the Homo Register? I'm getting sick of being picked up all the time.

— I'll see.

— Never mind that shit. In or out?

— All right. I'll take you out of it. Now, are you going to listen or not?

He could never understand how Freddy had done so well as a boxer when he couldn't keep his mouth shut. Boxers only had a minute between rounds. How could the seconds tell him how to win if he was chattering all the time?

— Sorry.

It was as if Freddy had read his mind. His tone was different, quiet and serious, and it caught McCarthy by surprise. He must have realised that McCarthy really meant what he said. — What do I do when I find her, ah, it?

— Ring the coppers. Oh, and make sure you walk all round the body. There have to be plenty of your footprints around it. Be up there about half past seven. Be going for a walk or something. But be there. Then barge over to someone in Marjoribanks Street and start yelling for them to get the coppers. Make a hell of a fuss. Keep out of Hawker Street.

— I'll need an excuse for being there.

— Bloody think of something. Don't you boxers go for training runs?

— Haven't been in a ring in years, Murray.

McCarthy shook his head. — Jesus bloody Christ, Freddy. Just bloody do it. Eight o'clock, all right. I'll be at Central. As soon as the panic gets going, your name comes off the Homo Register. Is that fair enough?

Freddy nodded. He was looking at the floor. McCarthy could see he was close to tears. — I've gotta say 'thank you' for taking me off the Homo Register.

He grabbed McCarthy around the neck, to hug him. McCarthy angrily pushed him back. — For Christ's sake, Freddy, what do you think you're doing! You're a poofter. Someone might see me! Jesus, you dropped your bloody marbles?

With that, McCarthy turned and walked out into the street. He did not look back. He walked back into Courtenay Place until he was a safe distance from the Taj Mahal. He brushed the front of his suit where Freddy had tried to hug him.

He kept walking. He knew what he was going to do. There was a busy night ahead, and tomorrow was going to be a long and difficult day.

chapter thirty-one

'Come on John!'

'All right, all right. I'm getting a move on!'

I think he is getting a bit tired of me always being the bossy older brother. He is definitely sick of me always provoking him before he does his First Communion confession, which he has to do so he is in a state of grace when he has his First Communion.

I want to see how many sins of yelling and swearing I can make him commit, so he has to do more confessions. He is getting fed up. John takes his First Communion very seriously.

'I'm ready,' he yells. I am not sure I believe him. It is half-past six in the morning and John is always a slow starter. It always takes him ages to get his clothes on and eat his toast and get down to the bus stop. Most times John is about one minute ahead of the bus, sometimes carrying his last piece of toast with him. The only times we can guarantee he will be on time is when it is raining. Wet toast is no fun.

This morning John surprises everyone. He really is ready.

I am going to the church with him, and will wait up at the back for him. Mum says that if I even think about causing any mischief it will take her about five minutes to get to the church and skin me alive.

I don't believe her. It takes a lot longer than that to get to the church. But I believe her about the skinning part. This happened before, when Richard O'Hanrahan and I sneaked into the church's sacristy, to see what altar wine tasted like. We found the bottle but had trouble getting the cork out of it without a corkscrew. The Communion hosts were all right. They were still in their packet, which meant they hadn't been blessed, because Richard said a blessing wouldn't go through a wrapping. I was not sure about that, because when people get blessed it's a blessing for their soul, and people are wrapped in skin. We didn't have time to have an argument about this, because we wanted to get on with eating boxfuls of the hosts.

The force of Catholic justice caught up with us the

next day. Our case for the defence got blown out of the sky because Richard's cap was found at the scene of the crime, and we had been seen sneaking into the sacristy. We got extra straps across the hands for taking the hosts and then for not admitting it. I thought you didn't have to make a statement if it would incriminate you, and they had to give you a formal caution that they were going to use your evidence against you. I didn't think I got justice, unless the law was different for police and priests and Marist Brothers.

Today is Wednesday, so John and his class are not the only ones getting their confessions told. Anyone can come along. But the only other people when we arrive are the three old ladies who turn up every week. Mum said once that they came along because they were widows and didn't get out of their houses all that much, and it was a chance to catch up with each other.

The nuns get the First Communion kids in neat rows near the confessional boxes, but behind the three old ladies. They always go first, even when the schoolkids are there before they arrive. I don't think that is fair because it is 'first come, first served' for everyone else. I say this to the nuns sometimes and the atmosphere gets a bit chilly. When they start remembering the names of the Communion thieves, it is time to shut up.

The door at the back of the church thumps open, and the wind blasts in. The man doesn't seem to care about that. He just keeps walking. He has a suit on, so he isn't a tramp or anything. He doesn't look very happy. His whiskers are starting to show, like they do on adults when they haven't had a shave for a couple of days. He is wearing a hat, which he keeps on.

The crease in his pants has gone, making his trousers look all baggy. He smells the same as everyone does at Christmas, beer and whisky.

He wobbles a bit when he flops down in the pew next to the confession boxes. The Sisters have always told us not to do that. They say it is a mark of respect to God to sit up with our backs nice and straight.

The old ladies do a bit of fluttering around when they see that he has pushed in front of them. He looks around to see who is whispering, and then looks to the front again. Still, it must have done some good because that's when he remembers to take off his hat. I recognise him then. It is Murray McCarthy. He is in the police, though he doesn't wear a uniform like Jerry O'Connell.

The old ladies are whispering again. He turns around. 'Look,' he says in a loud voice, almost yelling, 'you wanna go first? It's all right. I don't mind. I've got time. Time's what I've got, all right. I've got bugger all else.'

Father Reilly pops his head out from the sacristy door to see who is making all that noise in church. I am near the back so I can see the nuns nodding towards Murray McCarthy, and waving their hands at Father Reilly to hurry up and get going with hearing the confessions.

Father Reilly comes zooming out of the sacristy. I don't think I have ever seen him go that fast before. If he could do that all the time he could get a place on the wing in our soccer team. He seems to be picking up speed as he reaches the confessional box and dives into the middle space.

McCarthy stands up and waves at the old ladies. 'Go on! You want to go first. Off you go. Tell the priest all about it. Go on! Go on!' He is talking very loudly. This is a church!

Two of the old ladies get up and go into the confessional boxes on either side of the priest. The other one stands up and looks at McCarthy. 'You are rude!'

It is almost painful to hear her struggle to get the last word out. She grabs her handbag and walks out with her nose up in the air, trying to be as dignified as she can.

McCarthy's jaw drops. 'Jesus Christ. That's almost swearing. That's almost a fucking venial sin.' He looks around, and then up at Jesus on the crucifix. 'Sin everywhere, fucking sin every fucking where. Everywhere. Everywhere.' He drops his head down on his arms. 'Fucking everywhere!' His backside is on the seat and his shoulders are going up and down, as though he is doing big sobs.

The two old ladies come out of the confession box at almost the same time, which is strange. They must have had a combined confession. I didn't know you could do that. They don't stop and do their penance. They just put their heads down and take off for the door, with little sideways glances at McCarthy as they go. The other old lady, the one waiting for her confession, is up near the door and waiting for them.

McCarthy stands up and weaves into the confession box. Susan Hennessey, who is the first in line, gets up as we had all been taught to do and goes into the box on the other side of the priest, so no one wastes the priest's time.

We are all close enough to the confession box to hear him crash down on the kneeler and start bellowing, 'I wouldn't have a clue how long since I was in one of these. Father, I told the queer to go and find the body. I've been blackmailing him. I've been blackmailing people for years. But I've done much worse things. I've . . .'

Sister Ignatia jumps out of her seat, rips open the other confession box door, grabs Susan Hennessey by the hand and drags her back to the pews. Susan squeals, 'But Sister, I was in a state of contrition!'

Sister Ignatia isn't interested. 'I'm sure you'll be able to offer up your prayers and get into another state of contrition!' She looks back at the confessional. If everyone is hoping that it is going to be all of it they are wrong.

McCarthy is purging himself. 'We caught this old ex-prostitute doin' abortions for carnies. She was out the back of a billiard room and she was using knitting needles on 'em. We sprung 'er and told her the court might take pity on her, so she was goin' to start servin' her sentence right now. We stuck her over the table and we all fucked her. God help me, Father, I was standing there with a knitting needle in me hand and I was tellin' her what I was gonna do with it. Then we prosecuted her anyway, and we told her that if she said anything about getting rooted we were going to plant stolen goods in the house of every one of her relatives, anywhere in the country.'

The next bit is drowned out. It starts to rain, and the wind outside sounds like the makings of a full-on Wellington southerly. The rain is already coming down hard; thousands of drummers playing on the church's tin roof. The nuns look at each other and make their decision. They don't have to say a word. They start herding the children away from the confession boxes.

Sister Ignatia is nearest to the confession box. She pauses when McCarthy sobs out the names of people he let my Uncle Pat and his blokes beat up because they were behind on the payments for their betting. She leans close, trying to hear as much as she can. She looks angry.

McCarthy has moved on. 'We were taking money from the bookies. We were all in it, and that little girl got murdered up on Mount Victoria because of something to do with it. I bloody know it. I do. I bloody know it. Murdered, because we were bloody greedy for money! The fuckin' evil, Father. The fuckin' evil!' He sobs again. 'There's greedy coppers all over Wellington. It's a bloody growth, and I'm right at the fuckin' heart of it. I've fuckin' sinned, Father. I've fuckin' done it. I don't deserve anything.'

With that, Sister Ignatia gets very aggressive about getting the children, including John, who is working hard on getting into a state of grace, as far as she can from the confessional. She angrily whispers at the children, 'Heads down and pray to get in a proper state of contrition. Heads down and pray. Remember, we want you in a state of purity for your first confessions.'

The nuns pick this up, whispering at the children as the little heads bow in intense prayer.

I am right behind them, and notice that John has stopped praying. He is starting to get a lot more interested in hearing what is going on in the confession box, especially after Uncle Pat's name got mentioned. Then he realises that he is the only one not praying and he is surrounded by nuns. He has to give in then and start praying. His head bows and he obediently murmurs, joining the little buzz of bees extruding innocence.

By now McCarthy is yelling, mixing his yelling and sobbing, mixing the details of his life of corruption, illicit sex and thuggery with howls of 'I don't deserve it. I don't deserve to be here.'

Finally the door of the confession box opens and he is out, half-walking, half-stumbling towards the door, tears running down his face.

Father Reilly pokes his head out from the confession box in time to see McCarthy go out the door. His mouth is open; he looks dazed.

The kids at school all know it is worth three Our Fathers and three Hail Marys if you take someone else's lunch, or are disrespectful to your parents. Trying to decide what to give someone who sodomised an abortionist, or took money from bookmakers to corrupt other policemen, must put Father Reilly into a penance crisis. If he is going to be consistent, he will have given enough Hail Marys and Our Fathers to keep Murray McCarthy chattering out his prayers for the next three years.

chapter thirty-two

As soon as I get out of church I run all the way up Miramar Avenue back to Marist Miramar. I'm puffed when I get there, but it's good training for the game against Miramar North, which is only two weeks away.

When I get home I am going to ask about missing out some time from school homework to practise dribbling a soccer ball, taking free kicks and penalties. The Miramar North game is getting close. It's getting more and more important too, because if we win it might be the end of people yelling at us for being Catholics, and it might also mean we can get our Miramar Inquisition going.

Not a hope. My mum and Terry Taylor's mum and two of the other mothers from up the road are sitting in our dining room and drinking tea. It's hopeless even thinking about asking, because the atmosphere is not very happy. One of the mothers from up the road is crying. She is mopping her eyes with a handkerchief. My mum and Terry Taylor's mother have their arms around her shoulders.

Mum sees me and John standing there, waiting to find out what is going on. Not a chance. 'You and you, off up to your room and do your homework. I'll call you when I want you for dinner.' Mum is definite.

The door closes behind us. It must be a real emergency, because Mum forgets to wait till we are through the passageway and the next door has closed before she turns away.

That means we can listen! John and I immediately get on our knees so we can put our ears up against the door.

It doesn't take long to figure out they are talking about beer and husbands.

'If he does it again, you get the police.'

'Jerry O'Connell! He goes fishing with him!'

Mum chips in. 'If you want to, and you think he's going to hit you again, you can come straight around here. Bring the kids.'

'You haven't got any room. Not for me and three of them.'

'Nonsense. We've got so many kids here a few more won't be a problem. We'll just top and tail them. There's absolutely no problems at all, any time of the day or night.'

John and I don't like that idea. It's us who will get topped and tailed, us at one end of our bed and another kid up at the other end.

Terry Taylor's mum is also talking. 'If that doesn't work, or it's a bit far, you just come down to our place.'

That starts the other mother crying all over again. I'm not sure but I think she's a mum of someone who plays for Miramar North. This is annoying but it does not sound like a good time to rush in and start talking about traitors to Marist Miramar. If I do that, I can definitely forget about practising soccer.

Surely she must know the crying woman's son might be playing against us. If they win, he will be doing his bit for oppression over Catholics. We are being condemned to a lifetime of fights at the bus stop. Doesn't she have the slightest idea to what horror she is condemning her own children?

Then the women all start talking again. This time it is Terry Taylor's mum. She is talking about leaving Terry Taylor's dad. Hey, this is much better! Maybe Mum is more clever than I thought. If Terry Taylor's mum leaves his dad, he will have a lot more to worry about than attacking us. There's even a chance he might have to go and live somewhere else.

But no.

Mum says, 'I don't know. There's no help from anyone. Look what happens when someone is a widow. It's very lonely.'

I want to yell, 'Aw Mum, come on! Stop it. Separation's what we want!'

'I think you have to concentrate on the good parts and just let the rest go by,' she says.

There is a buzz as the women all agree with her.

I feel my shoulders sag with the disappointment. I was so close to seeing Terry Taylor's whole existence smouldering in ruins around him, and finish up with nothing. Mum could have shoved the knife in, and she let the chance go by!

Hearing her help save a marriage and give another little kid a proper home life is a sad, sad thing. John admits defeat and wanders off to get his books and start his homework. I decide to stay, crossing my fingers and toes that the women will all reconsider, especially Terry Taylor's mum.

Nothing.

I hear chairs scraping on the floor. They are getting up and leaving. I can hear Mum saying goodbye and the cups going in the basin. Normally she does the cleaning up, so I will have plenty of time to escape. Instead she opens the door. Too quick for me — I am caught standing there with my ear where the door had been.

I look up to see whether I'm going to get growled at.

Her eyes are a bit red. She has been crying. 'Don't drink beer to help with everything,' she says. 'It stops you being the person people married you for. That's a worried woman.'

Married me for? I'm only eight!

'Are you angry, Mum?'

She looks at me. I get a bit nervous, because she looks at me for a long time, not saying anything.

'Yes, a bit.'

'Is it me?'

'No, no, it's not you. But it could be you in about twenty-five years' time.'

This is interesting and I am keen to find out more, but she waves me away. She wants to get on with things. I head for the back door, hoping to kick my soccer ball around for a while.

'Denis.'

'Yes, Mum.'

'Homework!'

We might have been having some sort of crisis here, but it has definitely ended. This is business as usual.

It was a long way from business as usual with Dad. He was in the public bar of DeBrett's with Pat Conlin. It was Pat's last night in Wellington. At midnight the ship that would take him to Melbourne was to cast off. He was not expecting to come back.

He had asked Dad to have a final beer with him. Dad had thought that was very generous. He was now finding out why Pat had been generous — he knew Dad had been at sea and had travelled ringbolt back from Melbourne, and he wanted to know what was in store for him

Pat was nervous. He used to be a tough fighting man,

but too many nice dinners and too much beer had softened him up, and he knew it. 'I don't mind telling you, Kev,' he said, 'I'm worried. I get to the top of the stairs, any stairs, and I'm puffing. God, I went up to Ruby's house of harlots the other day. I tell you, it's a bastard now. By the time I climbed up there from The Terrace it was as much as I could do to service one of them. Time was, I could keep two of them going for a good three quarters of an hour.'

Dad nodded. He was hiding his distaste. These days he took his job as a Catholic father very seriously. He didn't like to hear stories like that any more. He had become an auditor. People relied on them to be strict and tough. They were not supposed to be people who spent their spare time drinking beer in pubs and hearing about having sex with two women at once.

'Now I'm off on this bloody tub to Melbourne.'

'So what's the problem?'

'I've got used to a bit of comfort, Kev. I don't know if I can go the rough stuff any more.'

Dad nodded, trying to hold back a smile. 'It'll be a bit rough.'

'Will I get a bed on my own?'

'Sort of.'

'Whaddya mean, sort of?'

'Well, they work shifts, six hours on, six hours off, right round the clock. Some ships have a system where one bloke uses the bed while the other one is working.'

Pat shuddered with revulsion. He didn't realise Dad was making it up, just to see the reaction. 'What happens if some bloke wants his bed back in the middle of the night?'

'My advice is to give it to him. Otherwise you could be cuddling up with a stoker. If you're lucky, you'll get one who's had a shower when he finished his shift. It makes them smell a lot fresher.'

'Aw Jees, Kev.' Pat was about to have another beer. The thought of cuddling a muscle-bound stoker stopped him cold.

Dad was starting to enjoy this. It was the first time he had ever had the advantage over Pat, who would normally destroy anything in sight to make sure he was always in control of any situation. It used to annoy Dad. Now he was in charge, and he was going to enjoy it.

It was easier than before. Ever since Frank Wilkins was fished out of Evans Bay, and Mary West disappeared from Mount Victoria, Pat was a different man: jittery, nervous and preoccupied. He had stopped concentrating on the business. Alex, who used to be the stand-over man for Arthur Cody and who still worked for Pat, started thinking it would be safe to kick Pat in the balls and tell him he had a brand new partner. There was no need. Pat was so distracted that the business was falling into his hands by default.

'Pat, there's something else.'

Pat looked at him, worried and not trying to conceal his fear.

'It's the stewards, Pat. Some of them might be able to find a bed for you. There might be one or two who would be extremely helpful, if you know what I mean.'

'Poofters! Jees, Kev, that's disgusting.' Pat's eyes

were wide open at the possible horror waiting on the ship.

Dad smiled. This was good fun. 'Just be a bit careful.' Pat held his breath. Dad was amazed. He had never, ever seen Pat like this. 'If you drop the soap in the shower it might be better to leave it, if some of the blokes have been at sea for a bit long . . .'

'Bloody hell, Kev. That's horrible.'

'And there's just one other thing. You might struggle a bit for regular tucker.'

Dad knew this would hurt. Pat had become famous for his love of fine cooking. He had recipe books posted from England so he could sample the very latest in international cuisine. Pat had just come out of a long 'brains and sausages' phase, cooking them in a thick, rough sherry.

'Struggle? Do I have to take my own stuff with me?'

'It might be an idea to take a few bits and pieces. A couple of loaves of bread would be good.'

'Don't they slip me a dinner or something? They'd better. I paid enough.'

'If the captain or the mate is sniffing around, they might have trouble smuggling stuff out. You'd miss out. Ringbolts are the bottom of the heap.'

Pat didn't say anything, just looked. There was real fear in his eyes.

Years later Dad would talk about that exact moment. He said it changed the way he thought about life. He stopped envying the way Pat lived, the way he made up his own rules, did whatever he wanted and whenever he wanted. He stopped admiring the things that had impressed him; the way people were afraid of Pat, and how his power reached right up and down to every corner of Wellington's life. Pat knew the rich and poor. He could do favours and wipe out debts. He could also get people hurt and killed. My Dad, working his way up in the different accounting sections of government departments, would remember his wild, free days at sea and think how much better his life had turned out.

Now Pat was looking as if he had suddenly got old. He was petrified of ending in Mount Crawford, waiting for other people to tell him the time and date he was going to die. His power and bluster had gone. No one would be frightened of this overweight man standing in a public bar worrying about whether he would get enough to eat on a small freighter, travelling to a city where no one knew him, and having to start all over again.

The only thing Dad would have liked was the money. Pat had organised a lot of it to be waiting for him in Melbourne. He had already checked. It was in the bank and he had the passbook.

That was when Dad decided that the way he lived was solid and good. It didn't matter that he had to struggle with having all those kids. There were Sunday nights when it was hard not to reach for another beer, knowing he would have to be on the 7.15am Fortification Road bus, and be all bright and ready for another working week. It might not be the most exciting life, but at this moment it became clear that it was better than the one ahead of Pat, once a buccaneer but now a nervous little man.

The two of them stood looking at each other. Without saying anything they lifted their glasses to salute each other.

'It's goodbye, isn't it Pat?' Dad said. He was serious now.

Pat nodded. 'I'm a bloody dinosaur now. It was good, but it's finished. I hope there'll be something in Australia.'

The two of them had another beer and shook hands. They stood for a moment, awkwardly wondering whether they should be like the Italians and hug each other. They couldn't. They were New Zealand men. They didn't do that sort of thing, not unless they wanted everyone to think they spent their nights hanging around the Taj Mahal.

The silence lasted for nearly twenty seconds. Pat broke it. 'See ya Kev.'

'Bye, Pat.'

Pat turned and walked away, past the two young policemen walking in to do a hotel inspection. They looked at Pat, and then at each other, trying to decide if he was someone they were supposed to talk to.

Dad shook his head. That was all the proof he would ever need that times had changed. Time was when Pat was known to every policeman in Wellington as someone who was a risk and dangerous to mix with. Now it was down to two pimply-faced coppers wondering who he was, and if he was anyone of interest.

Dad watched the policemen walking through the bar. He lifted his glass and drained it.

chapter thirty-three

Father Reilly was thoroughly fed up. The hostility and bad atmosphere which was persisting was going to drive him to drink. Father Bannon was still only talking to him on an as-required basis, and there did not seem to be any end in sight. He had to find something to do to escape. There was one thing he was not going to do, and that was stay here listening to the radio, to a New Zealand orchestra playing western hits, followed by a solid hour of *The Archers*.

Besides, there was something else which was much more important. That wretched bloody policeman had bleated out during his miserable ranting, self-pitying confession. In amongst the swamp of the confession there had been something about Catholic men getting caught in the Taj Mahal toilet, fallen among the sodomites. The poor men must be completely adrift from their Church to have found themselves in such a lonely, pathetic abuse of themselves and their bodies, and of others, having fallen to seeking a fleeting, ghastly pleasure in the vile acts of buggery.

If this was true, then these men needed to be saved. It was nothing less than a priest's duty to go out into the night and do what he could to bring them back to the warm, sheltering embrace of the Mother Church. Even more so if the alternative was sitting out here in Miramar listening to *The Archers* and waiting for Father Bannon to return to something near a human being again.

He opened the liquor cupboard and poured himself a triple whisky, throwing it down in one swallow. He shuddered as the liquor raced through him. He roared out a whisky breath, threw his head back and walked down the passageway to the front door, ignoring Father Bannon.

As soon as he was outside he sprinted to the little car, wanting to be on his way before Father Bannon realised what was happening. Two minutes later he was driving down Miramar Avenue, a priest of destiny on his way to rescue fallen Catholics. He kept checking the rear-vision mirror, hoping to see Father Bannon in the distance, shaking his fist and yelling at him to come home.

He parked the car a few yards from the Taj Mahal toilets, got out and looked around. The street was quiet. This was encouraging. So far he had not seen anyone from the Miramar congregation, the annual Corpus Christi march or, indeed, from the congregations at St Mary's of the Angels in Boulcott Street. He braced himself, set his shoulders back and marched to the Taj Mahal. He was going to perform his priestly function. He was going to save souls and redeem the fallen.

Father Reilly was not the only one thinking about doing his duty. Over on the other side of the road Jack Firth was standing quietly in the shadows beside the Central Fire Station. When he saw the man over the road — it was too dark to pick him as anything except an adult male — he began taking an interest. When Father Reilly looked around, presumably checking to see whether anyone was watching, Jack Firth began to move. — Good on you poofter, he muttered

As soon as Father Reilly disappeared into the Taj Mahal, Firth was standing beside the priest's car. He had a small screwdriver in his hand. Ten seconds later the passenger's door was open and Firth was lying across the seat, pulling wires out from under the dashboard. Fifteen seconds after that the engine was running and he was pulling in the driver's seat. This was not his personal best, but it was close.

In another five minutes he would be in Tory Street, at his brother's workshop. Four hours from now the little car would be repainted and down at the railway yards for shipping to Auckland. By midday tomorrow it would be re-registered and in their cousin's car yard. If they were lucky, the three of them would be splitting the profits by the middle of next week.

He stopped at the traffic lights, waiting for a line of three buses to go past. There was no one in front or behind him. He glanced over at the little glovebox, reached out and flicked it open. He swept its contents out onto the passenger's seat. Sometimes people left wallets and valuables there. If they had Jack's brother wouldn't be seeing any of them. Jack considered anything he found in the glovebox to be his personal bonus.

His bottom jaw dropped. A priest's prayerbook and one of those little hats with the tassels on top were on the passenger's seat. — 'Aw, shit. The homo's a bloody priest!

This was a shock for Firth. He liked priests, the only people who had ever treated him with anything close to kindness. He counted his three years at St Patrick's College the happiest of his life. For all he knew this might be one of the priests who had taught him at school. He had no choice. He had to return the car. It was a nuisance, but there were other cars and other nights. Besides, the Vauxhall he had stolen earlier was already being repainted. Money was being made.

He turned the car around, to see if the parking space was still empty. Two men jumped back into the shadows. Homos. Nothing to worry about there. He eased the car back into the parking place, and reconnected the wires so the priest could use his key to drive home when he'd finished. He got out, locking the door behind him.

He was grabbed by the collar and slammed face down on the car's roof. Another hand was grabbing his right wrist and twisting it up his back. Forget homos! Those two who jumped into the shadows were coppers. He knew skill when he felt it, and these two knew exactly what they were doing.

A voice was close up to his ear. — Bad boy, Jack. It's a night in the pokey for you.

He felt the policeman's grip loosen slightly. The two coppers were distracted, looking back towards the Taj Mahal. Father Reilly had tired of waiting for sodomites and was coming out for some fresh air to decide what to do next.

The two policemen waited till he had stopped beside his car. The bigger of them, Detective Sergeant Pat Connaught, asked, — Is this your car Father?

— Yes, it is. What's the matter?

— Get caught short, Father?

Father Reilly's reply was slightly huffy. — No, I wasn't.

— Can you wait here for a moment, Father?

The two policemen marched Jack Firth to a plain-clothes police car parked at the corner of Wakefield Street. His shoulders were slumped. If he hadn't done the right thing he would have got away with it.

Connaught smiled at the priest. Father Reilly noticed that the smile did not extend to the policeman's eyes. — Father, we'll get you to pop around to Central to help us out with a little bit of paperwork.

Connaught did not look like the kind of man who was going to take 'no' for an answer. Father Reilly decided to do what he was told. The policemen walked back to the police car, got in the driver's seat and drove off. Father Reilly followed them down Wakefield Street, towards Wellington Central in Waring Taylor Street.

When they got to Central, Jack Firth was escorted into the watch house and the cell block. Pat Connaught, keeping his grim smile on his face, gently steered Father Reilly to a small room in a corner of the CIB office.

As soon as Connaught was out of Father Reilly's sight, he sprinted down to the duty inspector's office. Thank God! He was in luck. Mick Mahon was there. That meant he wasn't going to have to hide Father Reilly from the Freemasons.

Mahon looked up as Connaught burst in. — We lifted Jack Firth from the Taj. He's been nicking the homos' cars again.

Mahon shrugged.

— The car we got him in belongs to a priest. Father Reilly, from Miramar.

Mahon stopped his paperwork. — Is he a queer?

— Dunno, but he came running out in a hurry when we were collaring Jack.

Mahon threw his pen down on his desk. — He do anything wrong? Did you see anything. Was his fly open or his cock out or anything like that?

— No.

— Good. Put Jack through for nickin' the car. Get a

statement off the priest. Make it sound like he was goin' somewhere, anywhere, except the Taj. No point feedin' him to the wolves if we can avoid it.

Connaught nodded and closed Mahon's door as he left.

Mahon fingered through the telephone book, stopping when he found the number for the Catholic diocese. He pulled the telephone closer, lifted the receiver and dialled.

No, the Bishop was not available. But the Bishop or one of his representatives would return the call.

— It's Inspector Mick Mahon from Wellington Central Police, and there's trouble with one of the priests.

— Hold the line a moment.

One minute later — Yes.

Mahon thought he recognised the voice. Not the Bishop, but someone very senior.

— It's Inspector Michael Mahon here. We have one of your priests here, Father Reilly, at Central. He was in the Taj Mahal toilets. It's a place where . . .

The voice cut across him. — I am aware of its reputation. Is the priest being charged?

— No, we just thought we'd mention it, because the circumstances could be, ah . . .

— Misinterpreted?

— Yes.

Mahon did not like the coldness in the priest's voice, and felt sorry for Father Reilly.

— Inspector, thank you. I am grateful you felt able to pass this on to me. I will deal with it, and I am sure there won't be any more problems. I'll organise things. Is it possible for him to telephone us?

— Of course.

— Thank you, Inspector. I am grateful and we are in your debt.

The line went dead. Connaught entered the office.

— What do you want us to do with the priest?

— Let 'im ring the Bishop, get his statement and get him out of here as fast as you can.

— All right.

— We won't have to worry about him. He's got caught by a much tougher police force than us. Now lean on Jack Firth to plead guilty to car conversion. Drop the charge down a bit, or promise to leave that thieving brother of his out of it. That might do the trick.

— What's the matter. I was hoping to fit them both up.

— Take what we can get. If this gets to a trial, I've got a feeling we might end up minus a star witness.

— The priest?

— The Catholics have been solving their problems longer than us. If I had a world-wide organisation I wouldn't be keeping him around here.

Connaught nodded and left the office. He couldn't care less about Father Reilly. He had just been given the green light to beat a guilty plea out of Jack Firth. Promise to keep away from his brother? Bugger that.

No one in Miramar saw Father Reilly again. Two days later he was on the flying boat to Sydney. A Customs officer named Mulvihill, a pillar of the Third Order of St Francis, saw him being collected by a couple of priests as soon as he passed through the Customs barrier. About a year later a letter turned up in Miramar, thanking us all for the help and kindness we had shown him, and doubting he would ever be back.

chapter thirty-four

It was one o'clock in the afternoon. Alice McCarthy sat on a little chair in the basement of her house, looking at Murray McCarthy lying on the earth floor. — Oh God Murray, what the bloody hell have you gone and done?

She could see what he had done. He'd killed himself by hanging from a beam in the small garage next to their house. His tongue had gone bright blue and was sticking out of his mouth, his eyes skewed up towards

the ceiling. He must have died before the rope broke.
One leg was under him and obviously broken. A large
wet patch spread over his trousers, where his bladder
had relaxed and emptied the half bottle of gin he drank
while working himself up to his end.

— You silly bugger, Murray. It doesn't matter what
it was. We could have sorted it out.

She bit her bottom lip, trying to hold her tears
back while she thought about the best thing to do.
Closing her eyes as she turned away, she opened
them once she was out of the garage. In the house
she dialled Wellington Central. Mick Mahon was off
duty and no, they would not be able to help with his
phone number.

She fished through Murray's address book and
found his home number.

Twenty minutes later his car was parked outside and
he was standing beside her, looking at the body. —
What am I going to do Mick?

The policeman looked at her with a keen, sharp gaze.

Alice looked back. — Whatever it is, I can do it Mick.

He nodded, taking her elbow and steering her out
of the garage. He padlocked it from the outside. — You
haven't rung anyone else?

— No.

— Good. That means it isn't officially reported yet.
Are you sure you're feeling strong, Alice? Do you want
a drink?

— No, Mick. I'll be all right.

— There's a couple of things you better know.

— He's hidden it at Central, hasn't he?

Mahon closed his eyes, not wanting to say anything. Then he nodded.

They drove to Wellington Central in silence. The only sound was Alice sniffing back an occasional tear. When they got to the corner of Featherston Street and Waring Taylor Street Mahon stopped the car. He took a key from his keyring, and smiled as he gave it to her. — It's the master key for every locker in Central. The troops don't know about it. Very useful it's been, too.

— Did you look in Murray's locker?

— No. Things were too complicated around Murray. Sometimes you were better off not knowing.

Mahon drove into the yard at Wellington Central. The 'Duty Inspector' place was taken. He parked in the space marked 'Commissioner'. He led the way up the stairs and along a corridor. He opened a door, looked in, and then gestured for Alice to enter. They walked past rows of lockers until they reached an unmarked one at the end.

Mahon tapped it.

— There you go, Alice. Quick as you can. I'll be outside. They won't get past me.

The key worked. There were uniforms hanging there. A pile of notebooks, shoe brushes, pens and bits and pieces. She knelt down and pushed the shoes aside. The floor of the locker moved slightly. She smiled. She felt around the edges, got a fingernail under a corner of the floor plate and lifted it. There was a steel box underneath. She lifted it out. It wasn't locked. Murray McCarthy had decided that if someone had gone to the trouble of finding the box, they wouldn't have any trouble unlocking it. She opened the lid, just enough to see the neatly stacked bank notes. She could see they were £20 notes, hundreds of them.

She pushed the clothes and shoes back into place and relocked her husband's locker. Mahon was still outside. He grabbed her by the elbow and whirled her around, so it would look as if she had always been walking down the corridor. He led the way back to his car and drove out into Waring Taylor Street, then right into Lambton Quay.

Alice was surprised. — Where are you going, Mick? Miramar's the other way.

Mahon did not reply. He drove down Lambton Quay, turned into Bowen Street and then left into The Terrace. He stopped the car. — Alice, I think there's a bit more you should know if you're up to it. The best time's now. When people find out about Murray there'll be a rush to cover their tracks.

She nodded. She would be strong. — Mick, I was with him for a long time. I can put up with a lot.

Mahon put the car into gear and drove up The Terrace, stopping just before the corner of Salamanca Road, glancing over at Alice to make sure she was coping. He decided she would cope. She'd been married to Murray McCarthy for twenty years. She had probably learned to cope with anything by now.

They got out of the car and crossed the road to climb the concrete steps leading to the front door of a big green-and-white villa. Mahon knocked.

The door opened. A big man with a dull meaty slab

of a face looked them up and down. — Yeah? We're shut and there's no one here.

— I want to see Ruby, Mahon snapped.

— Who are you?

— Mick Mahon.

The dull face took time to register this information. A small woman, who looked at least seventy-five, pushed him out of the way. — Git out of the way, Davey. This is Mr Mahon. He's special. Come in. Come in!

She wore bright red lipstick and had tobacco-coloured teeth. Her eyes were bright, inquisitive. They flickered when she saw Alice.

— This is Alice McCarthy.

— Murray's wife? Ruby had recovered. Her gaze was clear and disconcerting.

— Murray's widow.

Ruby had a lifetime of reacting quickly to bad news and fast-moving events. — I'm sorry. I'm sorry.

— No one knows yet.

Ruby flicked a shrewd look. — Oh, I see. You better come in the office.

She waved them to two chairs in front of an expensive-looking desk. The papers on top of the desk were in neat piles. It looked efficient and organised. — I was waiting. Murray was here about one o'clock this mornin' and he said there was goin' to be trouble. I'm sorry to have mentioned that.

Alice nodded. It was all right.

— I've got it sorted out. The old woman dropped to her knees, pulled aside a small coffee table and swished back the drapes behind it. There was a modern safe. She began twiddling its dial.

— He told me that everything that's anywhere else is for her. Ruby nodded at Alice. — This is for splittin' between the two of us.

Mick nodded. — That sounds like Murray. Alice, is that all right?

Alice nodded. Her agreement ended the tension creeping into the atmosphere.

Ruby turned back to the safe, opened it and pulled out a large packet. Mick Mahon helped her lift it up on the table.

Ruby waved him back, found some scissors and cut it open. Inside was a pile of banknotes.

— It's a lot of money. There's nearly £20,000 there, Mick. One way or another I'd say it came from Pat Conlin and his book.

— Pat's gone. Mick shrugged. — I heard he went ringbolt to Sydney.

— Melbourne.

Mick shrugged again. He didn't care where Conlin had gone, so long as he stayed there.

Ruby looked across the desk at Mahon. — Murray was right. Things is happening. They found that West girl this morning. You know who was right there on the scene? Freddy.

Mahon's eyebrows flicked up. — The boxer?

— The homo . . . and the boxer. There's dirty work there, Mick, and there's money in it somewhere.

— Ruby, can we have a talk about this another time? We've got to get on with it.

Alice looked up. — What do you mean, 'get on with it'?

Ruby leaned over and put a bony hand on Alice's arm. — This is a brothel and I've just retired. Now, you and me have to go off and see Jimmy O'Hara. You don't just walk into a bank with this sort of money and fill out a deposit slip. It needs lighter minds than ours, my dear. It needs lawyers.

Ruby separated the money into two piles. — How are we going to get it down to O'Hara's? It was a clear hint that Mahon should offer to drive them down The Terrace to O'Hara's offices, opposite Bolton Street.

— I can't take you Ruby. You're a brothel keeper. I can't be seen driving you around on my day off!

Alice McCarthy took a deep breath, trying to comprehend all this. Her husband, still lying dead on the garage floor, had left £20,000 in the safe at a brothel. Now she was off to some lawyer's office, and she would end up with £10,000 of it. She had that and more in the box under Mick Mahon's arm. They would never believe this at the next Townswomen's Guild tea and scones morning.

— So we've got to walk!

— 'Fraid so, Ruby.

Ruby smiled. — I ain't putting this in any bag. All it'd take'd be someone to grab it and that's me house on the beach in Tauranga gone. When I go out, Mick, that's the end of it. I'm not coming back.

— What about the house?

— It's not mine. That bastard of a husband of mine left it to the Labour Party when he died. As soon as I move out it's theirs. I can't sell it and I can't get no money out of it. I've got no kids. The last one died in that car crash a few years ago.

The policeman nodded sympathetically.

— The girls who work here will survive. Davey, big useless fool that he is, can go try himself on some honest work. Is that box under your arm more money.

Mahon nodded.

Ruby was in charge. — Let's have it. Off you go. Go on, out!

She took the box and gave it to Alice, pushing the door closed in Mahon's face.

Ruby looked at Alice, trying to project as much kindness as she could. — You hold yourself together, my girl. It won't be long. Stand up, my darlin'. It's going in your step-ins. Come on. There's not time for modesty.

Ruby and Alice hoisted up their dresses, pulled out the elastic of their step-ins and dropped the money into their underwear. When they finished both women had a distinctly pear-shaped look.

Ruby opened the door. Mahon looked at the two women and smiled.

— That's enough of your smirking, Mick Mahon. You can drive along behind us, and you can keep your distance.

Ruby was giving orders now.

The two women waddled out into the passageway, towards the front door. Ruby was pulling on a pair of white gloves and attaching a hat covered in flowers to the top of her head.

Davey appeared in the doorway, blocking their way.
— What's going on?

— You can get out of the way! And you can tell the girls when they come in that the shop's closed. They all knew when they came to work here that might happen. Now it has. You can go and get a job. You've been stealing from me long enough, so I don't have to worry about you no more.

— You never warned me!

— It'd confuse you, Davey.

— You owe me money.

— You've stolen enough for about fifteen years of holiday pay.

Davey blocked their way. His chin was sticking out. His legs were apart. He was ready for trouble. Mahon eased between the two women. Davey put his hands up to push him away. Mahon ducked Davey's push, reached down, grabbed his testicles and squeezed. Still keeping his grip he lowered Davey to the floor, gesturing with his head for the two women to step past.

Ruby led Alice past a moaning Davey. — I'm supposed to look back, she said. — But I can't. I don't know there's all that much I want to remember from there.

They heard a dull thump. Mahon had made sure that Davey wouldn't follow them, by kicking him in the ribs.

The two women turned left at the bottom of the stairs, setting off down The Terrace towards Jimmy O'Hara's office. The money stuffed under their dresses made them look like two gently swaying and delicately off-balance freighters elegantly slicing through choppy water.

chapter thirty-five

James O'Hara was leaning forward, listening to his secretary asking him if she could have an afternoon off. — No. We are far too busy. We've got all this Law Society stuff to get away. If you took off today we'd be straight into a crisis.

The secretary scowled, flashing him an angry look as she closed the door a fraction too vigorously behind her. O'Hara shook his head. Things weren't going to be much fun around there for a day or two.

When he looked out the window he nearly fell off his chair. Walking towards his office were three people he never, ever expected to see together in any combination ever: Murray McCarthy's wife, Ruby McNamara and Mick Mahon. He jumped to his feet, jerked open his office door and snapped at his secretary.
— Things have changed. Have the afternoon off, but go out the back way, right now.

She grabbed her bag, gloves and hat and hared towards the office's back door.

O'Hara waited. This was going to be interesting.

The visitors pushed through the door. O'Hara was in the outer office to meet them. He waved them through to his office, and made sure the door was closed behind them.

A minute later, Mick Mahon was enjoying being there at the first time Jimmy O'Hara could not think of anything to say. The two women were unloading the contents of their step-ins on his desk. Alice McCarthy added the money from the box from her husband's locker. Mahon's guess was over £30,000. It was actually £35,000. By comparison, the McCarthy five-bedroom house in Miramar was worth £7,000.

O'Hara flopped back in his chair, shaking his head. Mick Mahon struggled to hold back his laughter. — I think the ladies would like some investment advice, Jimmy.

— I think they do. I do suspect you might be right.

Mahon eased Alice forward. — Can you look after Alice first? Her husband's just died, and when we are finished here we're going out to her place to discover the body.

O'Hara nodded. He had a career based on making perfect sense of statements like that. He ushered Mahon and Ruby out to his secretary's desk, then sat Alice McCarthy down and began talking to her, quietly and seriously, about the investment of large sums of money.

In the foyer Ruby and Mahon sat in silence for a moment. Mahon spoke first. — You really finished, Ruby?

— Yup, and I know what you are thinking. You want my diaries and a list of the clients.

— It might be useful.

— Gawd, Mick, you can guess most of them.

— True enough. What are you going to do now?

— I've got a little place a couple of miles south of Tauranga, right on the beach. There's a little balcony. I can't think of a better place to sit with a nice cool gin and watch the sun go down over the sea. I'm done, Mick. I'm too old. I never realised that Davey was stealing so much. I ought to have gone years ago.

— Before you go, Ruby, I want you to make a formal complaint about him.

— Wouldn't do any good.

— There's a clean-up coming. We're moving into different times. It would do some good. Was he paying coppers?

She nodded.

— Is he mixed up with reefers or the bookies?

— Reefers, but I'm not sure about bookies.

— I'll look after him. I'll supervise it personally. You never know. You might get a bit of your money back.

— I'm seventy-six, Mick. I don't need money, not now.

— It's the principle. You can always give it away.

— Thanks, Mick. You were always a good man.

Mahon leaned back and sighed. — I might not be too far behind you. Nearly thirty years of working in the sewer's close to enough for me too.

Ruby sighed. — It gets to you. I can't ignore the pain in the girls' eyes. They never get over turnin' themselves into a prostitute, no matter what they say. It's always with them, like a mark of Cain.

She stopped, and smiled. — Gawd, listen to me. I never thought I'd finish up spoutin' the *Bible* at coppers. Still, it's true. I seen hundreds of them. None of 'em went out better than when they came in.

Mahon didn't say anything. He didn't want to interrupt. In all the years he had known her, this was the most she'd ever said to him.

She was still in a mood to talk. — The ones I always felt for was the girls that ran off with sailors on the ships. I knew a lot of 'em that went off to other countries. They all said they'd write to me. None of them ever did. Not one.

Mick nodded, letting her talk.

— Girls and sailors cooped up on a ship for weeks. It's trouble, Mick. One sailor's got the girl. Another one wants her, just like something you take off the shelf in a shop. There's drink and there's knives.

— Bad mix. Mahon muttered encouragingly.

— I bet it ended with them sailors and the girls cut up, and them sailors slipping the bodies over the side when no one was looking. Or she ends up getting chucked over the side. That's the worst, Mick. Imagine what it's like bein' in the middle of the Tasman or the South China Sea, and in the dark of the night watching the ship sailin' away and keepin' going till you can't move any more, or the sharks come for ya.

She took a breath. — Or they get taken off by the police in some horrible hot country, and that's the end of them. They wasn't bad girls. They made some mistakes and it went from bad to worse, and they was trapped.

Mahon nodded his head sympathetically.

— And you know what, Mick? I spent my life making money off them. It's not easy to live with, not now. I could cover it up once, pretend it was none of me business. I can't look into them dull eyes any more. I can't take away any more hope.

Mahon sat up. This was interesting. It gave him an idea. If Ruby wanted redemption then he might be able to help. — When were you goin' up north?

— I'm not going back to the house. Thought I might as well keep going.

— I have got something to ask you. It might take a day or two. What about treating yourself to the best room at the St George? I'm sure you've got a bit more money tucked away than's in there.

Ruby smiled at him. He was right.

— I've got a little job, and you might enjoy it.

— I'm not giving no names, no matter what.

— No, no, no. Conlin's gone, but I think there might be a few others getting ready to try their luck. There's a bit of trouble out in Miramar.

She cocked a shrewd eye at him. — Spit it out you fat bugger.

Mahon smiled his soft little smile.

Ruby looked at him. — You talking about getting Errol in there somewhere. I thought you hated him and that newspaper of his.

— God's work, Ruby. It's all God's work.

Ruby's chuckles rolled around her jowly face. — Might be a bit of entertainment for a day or so, then I'm off.

Mahon nodded his agreement.

— I'll miss you, Mick.

— It was interesting having you around, Ruby.

O'Hara's door opened. Alice McCarthy came out. Although she was smiling, her face was white. Mahon guessed she could not take much more. O'Hara nodded to him: all was well.

Mahon took her by the elbow and sat her down in a chair. — You stay there. I'll get the car, and then we'll take you home and we'll discover Murray. I'll look after everything. It'll be all right.

As he pushed open the door to leave, he saw her drop her head in her hands and her body begin to shake with sobs.

chapter thirty-six

This is another bus-stop drama
coming up the hill towards us. Terry Taylor looks as if
he's in a bad mood. We get ready for anything, fists
clenched and ready to go. We have even learned off a
whole lot of abuse about Protestants if he starts saying
anything about Catholics.

His eyebrows are knotted together and he is looking
absolutely straight ahead, almost not seeing us. That
suits us. Then we get a real surprise. He just walks

straight past us. There is no punching, no yelling, no abuse, no nothing.

He turns the corner into Nevay Road, and he still hasn't said or done anything. It must finally have got too much for him. Just before he gets out of shouting range, he turns back and yells at us, 'We're gonna beat ya in the soccer.'

This is all! It's really mild. There are some adults standing there waiting for the bus, including the man who works at the quarry. None of them takes any notice of us. They decided boys yelling at each other about a soccer match is nothing to get excited about. Typical adults, really dumb.

This was different from Terry Taylor. I wonder whether it is anything to do with his mother talking about leaving his father. Just then our bus comes around the corner. We all get on and it takes off. Terry Taylor looks up when we go past him. He glances up, then just keeps plodding along the road. He doesn't look very happy. John and I are trying to figure out what's gone wrong. Maybe it is because his mother has been drinking tea with Mum and it has ended with the Protestant Scourge, which has only one member so far, and that's Terry Taylor, not being allowed to yell at us any more.

We remind ourselves to be on extra-special alert. Maybe he is planning something, and trying to get us all relaxed, so we won't be ready when he springs whatever surprise he is planning.

Sister Ignatia wasn't ready, and doubted whether she would ever be ready, for the magnificent figure sweeping up to the front door of the nuns' house. Ruby was dressed in her colourful best, including a hat wide enough to shelter at least two other people. She had been too enthusiastic with the face powder and the bright red lipstick. She was wearing her best shoes, with their too-high heels, causing her to totter slightly on the rough concrete.

She knocked on the door. — I am Ruby McNamara.

— I am Sister Ignatia. Come in.

Yes, Ruby would love a cup of tea. She would also get straight to the point. — I heard you got a bit of trouble here in Miramar, with men bein' bastards, with bettin' and beer.

Sister Ignatia only just managed to stop herself from spilling her tea. — Well, yes, there are problems.

— Right then. Ruby wasn't going to waste effort on pleasantries. — I'm not here to take up your valuable time. But getting men to behave is how I've been earning my living for the last thirty years.

— Have you been a teacher?

— No, I ran a brothel.

— Oh. Would you like another cup of tea?

— No. Ruby wanted to sail onwards.— I came out to help you to get them to behave a bit better. A friend of mine thought I might be able to help.

— Who is . . .

— Mick Mahon. He's a policeman.

— Yes, I have heard of him.

Ruby had had enough of the preamble. — The trick with men doing things they shouldn't is they are always desperate to keep it secret. I saw that all the time in the brothel. They'd wipe their little boys on the sheets and tuck them back in their pants.

Sister Ignatia nodded, wondering what could possibly be next.

— And then they'd go off home to be model parents in places like this. They're always the first to climb on any morals campaign, especially against workin' girls who have to have sex for their bread and butter.

Ruby stopped. — I'm sorry to be talking like this, with you being religious and everything, but I thought it would be better to get off to a clear start.

Sister Ignatia nodded a complete if slightly bewildered agreement. The bit about the sheets might have been more detail than she needed.

— You gotta expose them. Not their little cocks, you understand, but their behaviour. It's the only way to stop slygrogs and bettin' with bookies and getting in debt and women getting beaten up when they complain. You gotta slow 'em down. You'll never stop vice. It's too exciting, but you can make it so risky they stay home and suffer instead.

— The police have been telling me . . .

— Never mind the coppers. Half of them are mixed up in it anyway, one way or another. This is a problem for women, and it's women's gotta stop it.

Sister Ignatia sat still, fascinated.

— Now and again ya gotta be prepared to get a man to help, even a useless bastard like Errol out there in the car.

— Errol? Sister Ignatia asked.

— Errol Finnegan. He works for *Truth*, calls himself

the fearless ace investigative reporter, and the ally of the people against the dark forces. Load of bloody rubbish. He'll print anything you tell him, long as it's grubby enough. He's one of youse. He's got three little girls at the Star of the Sea School in Seatoun. He thinks two of them might end up as nuns.

— I am sure they will be most welcome. They will certainly add . . . something. He's said he'll help?

— Bloody oath he will. I didn't give him a choice. He's out in the car right now.

— It might be an idea if I talk to the Reverend Mother.

— That's the stuff. But I'll introduce you to Errol anyway.

As she put her hand on the doorhandle she turned back to Sister Ignatia. — I don't know if I ought to mention this, Sister, but you better keep an eye on Errol. He's a bit of a sheet-sniffer, if ya know what I mean. Don't let him get near any of your bicycles, she said, tapping her nose.

Sister Ignatia didn't have the faintest idea what Ruby meant, and did not want to dwell too long on it either.

Errol Finnegan was a surprise. Sister Ignatia had been expecting someone much seedier-looking. He might have been a military colonel, strong-looking and immaculately dressed.

— Tea? Sister Ignatia asked.

Finnegan radiated a polite, crisp efficiency. — No thanks. Unfortunately we are a fraction squeezed for time, so I wonder if we could get down to business.

Everyone sat down. Finnegan spoke first. — It's very simple. If you find out where the slygrogs are, or the loan-sharking, or the betting places, we'll break them open, and there'll be no question of your name appearing anywhere. Not a dickybird.

Sister Ignatia nodded. — We can find out. The children talk in the playground. We were going to go to the police.

— Sadly, Sister, that's a bit of a waste of time, Finnegan purred.

— Waste of journalism prizes too, eh, Errol? Ruby grinned from the sidelines.

— *Truth*'s the paper and *Truth* is the place, Sister. We understand these things, and we can help as no one else can.

He reached into a pocket and handed Sister Ignatia a card. — Call me any time. It might be better to meet me at night, less eyes and ears around when the good people are all curled up in front of their wirelesses. All you have to do is tell me and I'll be there.

He stood and shook Sister Ignatia's hand.

— Remember, shame the bastards, said Ruby. — That's what stops them. Shame. Nothing like it.

Before Sister Ignatia could say anything, Ruby was tottering her way down to the car. She got in, slamming the passenger's door and nodding for Finnegan to drive off. She did not look back towards the nuns' house. She did not look back at anything in Wellington until she was in her first class berth on the night train to Hamilton. She would change there for Tauranga. She did not look back until she was past Titahi Bay and Wellington was well out of sight.

chapter thirty-seven

          This was the eighth time Errol Finnegan had waited patiently in the cold in the alleyway between the Holy Cross School and the priests' house. He stamped his feet to keep warm. It was so dark he could hardly see the time on his watch. He guessed it was about 11.30. He was starting to find these late nights harder and harder to cope with. He shivered. He was getting too old for this. Unfortunately he did not have much choice. The leads the nuns had been providing were turning out to be pure Grade A, government-certified perfection. So far he had exposed three slygrogs, two bookmaking rings, a loan-sharking operation and a brothel.

The only hitch in all this journalistic sunshine had been a certain amount of unpleasantness with Jimmy O'Hara, who had been unnecessarily specific about the years of litigation waiting if Ruby McNamara's name was besmirched by an appearance in any story. O'Hara also mentioned other matters lurking in his files.

Finnegan was then told that naturally fearlessness in journalism was all, and that nothing mattered except providing their readers with the truth. Naturally, this would mean concentrating the blame for the now-closed Terrace brothel's on a bewildered and angry Davey.

In Tauranga, Ruby McNamara sat on her balcony, chuckled as she read the coverage and drained the first of the day's gin and tonics. Then she telephoned Jimmy O'Hara, telling him to deduct his fee from the envelope of cash kept in his safe for these little emergencies.

Finnegan had filled out the Terrace expóse with photographs of two minor public servants fleeing, their hands held up to ward off the camera. From Finnegan's point of view this was excellent, because it added a sense of drama and you could still see their faces. *Truth*'s reputation for exposing sinners was safe.

At last he could see the two nuns ghosting up towards him. — Sisters!

— Hello, Mr Finnegan.

It was the Reverend Mother, who normally joined Sister Ignatia for these meetings. He would prefer she didn't use his name, in case she somehow let it slip in some other conversation.

— I have kept bigger secrets than that, Mr Finnegan.

Finnegan had been quite interested in the precise nature of these secrets. She kept those secrets too. He knew he would have more than enough to occupy himself when he saw the quality of the material the nuns delivered — They were taking this opportunity to strike out at vice seriously. All the teachers in the Catholic schools had been running sessions of morning talks. The little freckle-faced, front-tooth-missing innocents stood in front of their classes and willingly poured out everything happening at home. Teachers watched and listened for the key words 'bookie', 'bookmaker', 'loans', slygrog' 'prossies' and 'carnie'. If a child uttered any of these they would be bathed in support and praise, and be given another chance for a morning talk, often surprisingly quickly afterwards.

If a nugget of real sin was mined, details went to the Reverend Mother. Informal cross-checking led the Sisters to pinpoint Wellington's precise sources of sin. Distressingly, this seemed to involve considerable numbers of otherwise-good Catholics. A certain amount of discreet culling of information was necessary. One or two priests were given to spending an amiable hour or two with parishioners who were running slygrogs. Finnegan was not burdened with these details.

— We don't have as much as you would like this week, Mr Finnegan, said the Reverend Mother. — We do have the address of a slygrog in Island Bay, though.

She handed over a piece of paper. Finnegan glanced at it. It was on The Parade, not far from The Esplanade. Someone was brave, running a slygrog so close to the shops.

— We can't confirm it, Mr Finnegan, but we understand that place also has girls working there, and there are men in public life who visit there.

Slygrog, girls, politicians. Finnegan's hand shook with the excitement. — How do you know?

— We know, Mr Finnegan, the Reverend Mother answered. — We heard a distressing report that a young Catholic mother might have been trapped in that life, in that place.

Finnegan's hand trembled. A young Catholic mother fallen prey to politicians' filthy appetites. This was disgusting and must be remedied. Thousands of extra copies will be sold.

— There is just one other thing, the Reverend Mother said. — We were thinking that perhaps *Truth* might like to make a contribution to the school funds.

Finnegan had been waiting for this, and had his answer ready. — Look, Reverend Mother, I don't think *Truth* would be able to do that. We don't pay for stories. We're helping you get what you want, exposing crime and vice. I'll ask, but I don't think our editor will budge. It's a firm policy.

—You won't help us?

—Not won't. Can't. It's the paper's policy.

— You can't change the policy?

— I can ask, but I would doubt that they will do it. Finnegan shook his head in great sorrow.

The nuns bowed slightly to Finnegan, turned without another word and swept away to their house. They were not surprised. They had already known the answer. One of the women who helped sew the vestments had a sister-in-law who worked in the *Truth* accounts department. She had heard the editor saying to Finnegan that it might be an idea to look after the nuns, for all the good stories pouring *Truth*'s way. Finnegan's reply had astonished her. — No, fuck 'em. We're cleaning up the city for them. The Church has got a ton of money. Let it look after them. Maybe we should start having a closer look at them!

The editor, who did not particularly care either way, shrugged his shoulders. If Finnegan felt this strongly about it, let him have his way. Besides, as Finnegan pointed out, the flow of information was slowing. Maybe there wasn't much left.

Two nights later Errol Finnegan eased himself into as comfortable a place as he could find in the shrubbery outside the little Island Bay house. From there he could just see the outlines of some of the Italian-owned boats out in the bay. He could also see the people in the house. He peered hard, trying to recognise them.

He clutched his camera and edged in closer, gradually reaching a ground-floor window. Two women were doing a striptease for an audience of about six men who were holding open beer bottles and drinking from them.

Seamy, degraded and perfect.

He would have to hold on a bit longer, until at least one of the women was naked from the waist up. He wanted a photograph of her breasts.

He lifted the camera. He did not take his picture. Two men had grabbed him and spun him around. He tried to shove them off, but they anticipated him. He was flicked between them and flattened down in the soil. Handcuffs were slipped around his wrists. He was lying on the ground, his arms trapped behind him. A mouth came up close to his ear. — Make a sound and we'll kick the shit out of you and then we'll forget you're here for a couple of hours.

Finnegan nodded. He did not have much choice except agree with whatever they said. One of the men reached down and held his nostrils. As soon as he gasped for breath a strong hand shoved a handful of soil in his mouth. He was rolled round on his stomach and left to spit the dirt onto the ground.

Finnegan blinked. People were quietly trampling their way past him. One of the men who had handcuffed him gave a wave. He must have been in charge. Suddenly there was noisy chaos. The police had kicked open the door, were climbing through the windows and fighting with the men trying to escape. Four young policemen elbowed each other out of the way in the scramble to arrest the now bare-breasted women.

Finnegan spat out the last of the dirt and swore. Then something truly frightening happened to him. A hand flicked his braces loose. He tried to lash out with his feet. Too late. Hands were pulling his trousers down over his shoes and socks. Now someone was hauling him upright. He saw someone in front of him. Oh God, no! It was a newspaper photographer. The flash blinded him. He blinked. Pop. Another photograph. — One more Errol, for the Christmas card! called a chuckling voice from behind the camera.

He stood there in his long-john underpants, suit jacket, collar, tie, socks and shoes as the photographer fired four more shots.

The police began to drag people out of the house. The reporter gently laid Finnegan back on the ground. — Sorry about that Errol, but you know how it is.

The reporter and photographer slipped away to their car, taking no interest in the raid, and drove off up The Parade, back towards the city.

Over on the other side of the road Sister Ignatia and Mick Mahon watched the police emptying the slygrog. — What happens now? she asked.

Mahon smiled. It's a win for almost everyone. The slygrog's finished. Our friend Finnegan's going to be well and truly humiliated, which he has been doing to policemen for years.

Sister Ignatia looked at him.

He blushed. — I made a bit of a mistake one night, going to Ruby's a few years ago and Errol saw me, and I've been hearing about it ever since. The photographer is from the *Dominion*, and he'll pass the photos along to the *Evening Post*. I'm sure the *Truth* editor will hear about this. So you might get something for the school fund. You never know.

chapter thirty-eight

It is a disaster, and it's happening on the morning of the most important soccer game in our lives, the one which decides who rules the Miramar Peninsula, Miramar North's Protestants or us, the Catholics.

It starts when John and I are sitting at our back door. John sees it first, the next-door neighbour's cat sitting there with a frightened little mouse scuttling around in front of it. The mouse keeps trying to escape. Every time it tries the cat reaches out a paw and flicks it back.

John has never had a pet mouse, and he wants one. The only thing we need to do is get the cat away from the mouse and it's ours. So John reaches out to grab the mouse. The cat doesn't like that. It puts one paw on top of it, pinning it to the concrete. The mouse has its legs going as fast as it can, to try and get some traction so it can escape. The cat's paw is firm. The mouse is staying where it is.

John reaches for the mouse again. It is a terrible mistake. He should have been looking at the cat's other paw. Too late. It happens fast. John has three neat red lines down the front of his face, across his eyes and down his cheek. He falls back, hurting his wrist as he tumbles.

We go home to get help for John's wrist and his scratches. Mum paints antiseptic down the scratches and says she will take him down to the doctor. John looks nervous. He doesn't look like a star soccer player. He looks more like a nervous little boy.

She hugs him. 'I don't think you need to make out your Last Will and Testament.'

'What about some lollies?'

'You will *definitely* survive!' Then she unloads the death blow: 'But you won't be playing soccer this afternoon.'

John doesn't look too pleased to hear that. On the way to the doctor, he whispers, 'I'll talk Brother Brian into it. He'll see it my way.'

An hour later Brother Brian is looking at John. 'Don't be absolutely ridiculous. You've got about ten pounds of bandages on that arm. And that could be an infection on your face. You are not playing.'

'But . . .'

'No buts.'

Brother Brian does offer one little compromise. If John stops grumbling, he can come to the soccer game and watch instead of staying back at the school and doing essays and sums.

'But Dad said the cat's a psycho, a completely mad cat, and it's owned by some Methodist people, who are nearly Protestants. You said in the boxing lessons we should never give in to Protestant bullies.'

Brother Brian is impressed with this. First, that John managed to get all that out in almost one sentence. Second, that John has remembered his homily about giving in to bullies. He can also see where this is going.

John looks at the expression on his face, and fires off another salvo. 'If the cat is a bully and it knows it has got away with bullying me, it'll only get encouraged to do it again. That's wrong, and it'll end up growing up all twisted and horrible and have a life of crime and end up in jail.'

Brother Brian is even more impressed with this. He makes a mental note to mention John's debating skill to Mum and Dad at the next parent/teacher night, but says 'No, I'm afraid you can't play. And you know what happens to boys who are disobedient.'

John looks up, all solemn and wide-eyed. 'They go to hell, Brother!' He is outgunned and knows it.

That leaves John standing glumly on the sideline

at Miramar North School. The referee waves the teams into the middle of the field. He gets the captains together and tosses the coin. We win and decide to play into the wind, so it will be behind us later when we are tired.

There are lots of mothers on the sidelines. I will know what they are talking about, because I am picked to play on the wing, which means I will be running up and down beside them all through the second half. That's also something which is wrong. They are all on the same sideline. They are supposed to be on opposite sides, the Catholics on one and the Protestants on the other. If the adults are divided it will make it easier when we win and we start the religious persecution.

The game has just started when Mrs Costello yells, 'Keep going, spread out. Remember what I said, spread out.'

One of the Protestant mothers standing near me laughs to her friends. 'That's what I did eight years ago, instead of having a headache, and that's why I'm here in the freezing cold watching my little beloved one making a mess of being a halfback.'

Their halfback looks around to see who is laughing. I am throwing the ball in, so I throw it straight at him. He traps it and kicks it miles up the field. Bad mistake. The mother must be talking about their other halfback. None of the mothers hear me say 'Damn,' because they are all still chuckling. The play is over on the other side, so I can see what's going on. It is not good. There are signs of peace breaking out. The Protestant mothers are starting to talk to the Catholic ones.

Mrs Costello has the right idea. She is standing apart and yelling at us. 'Watch out for Number One!' That is the code word for the move John and I saw Miramar North working on: passing the ball back to the fullback, who kicks it over to the winger, who crosses it, and their centre-forward scores.

She is trying to tell us they are doing their move. Unfortunately, by the time we realise what is happening they have already done most of it, and done it perfectly too. Their centre-forward is swinging back to meet Terry Taylor's cross. He traps the ball and lets fly. Our goalie is terrified of the ball hitting him on the face and smashing his glasses. He jumps out and turns his back on the centre-forward. The ball flies at him, hits his backside and blasts straight into the back of the net. It is 1–0 to them.

Terry Taylor stands there with a big grin. He looks as if he is getting ready to say something nasty to us. He sneaks a quick look to see if his mother is looking before he says anything. She is glaring at him, so he gives us this horrible big grin instead.

John looks even more glum. Mum puts her arm around him. I watch this, to see if he is going to shake her off in case he gets seen getting cuddled in front of the whole soccer team. He doesn't seem worried. He is happy to get a cuddle. For him it is something good in a bad day — getting torn apart by the cat, getting banned from the soccer game, and now we are losing.

Mrs Costello is still yelling 'Come on, Marist. Keep spread out. Keep moving. Pass the ball to each other!'

I pass to Micky Marsline. He gets clear and he can

see the gap opening up in front of him. He fires at the right-hand side of the goal. His shot hits the post and bounces over their line for a goal kick. This is the first time we have been properly on attack.

Mrs Costello leaps in the air, waving her hands in joy, but the referee blows his whistle. She yells 'What's that for? What's going on?'

He looks at her and says, 'You, madam. Look around. You are on the edge of the penalty area, and unless you change into a uniform and start playing I think you might be better off on the sideline.'

She looks a bit embarrassed and gets off the field, walking backwards, still yelling encouragement to us.

When the game starts again the wind drops, which makes it easier for us to get distance on our long kicks up the field. That doesn't mean we are going to get the ball in their goal. It just means they have to keep their fullbacks a little further back. Their team is starting to cram up together and it's getting difficult to tell where their forward line starts and their half-line ends.

Mrs Costello can see this, and yells for us to 'get it out wide, get them out wide'.

I get out wide, on the touchline near the mothers. One of them, a different Protestant one, is saying, 'If she tells those young men that just once more, I'm going to get very worried!' The other mothers, both the Protestant and Catholic ones, are chuckling and laughing at that. Mrs Costello says, 'I'm only working from memory, decades back.' The mothers all laugh again.

Just then the referee blows the whistle for the end of the first half. Twenty minutes have gone, just like that!

The mothers, who had been gradually forming one group, instead of doing what I wanted, which is staying in Protestant and Catholic camps, split up to go off and get the oranges.

As we are walking off, Terry Taylor walks past me and drops his shoulder into me, knocking me backwards.

'See, we're beating ya, ya Catholic dogs.'

This is a mistake. His mother is standing behind him.

'Terry!'

He looks round. His mum is frowning. 'That's enough of that. Say sorry to Denis!'

This is horrible for both of us. He doesn't want to apologise, and I am quite happy to barge into him when the game starts again, and get even that way.

'Go on!' she orders.

'Sorry,' he grumps.

Mum is standing behind me. 'Say thank you to Terry for apologising.'

This is getting worse. 'Thank you for apologising,' I mutter. Both of us, feeling insulted and beaten, are finally able to get away and get our oranges.

Mrs Costello tells us, 'You've got to get out to every corner of the field so they have to run after you.' We nod, and don't say much. This is because we're all counting the pieces of orange to see if there are enough for two pieces each. If not, someone will miss out, and there will be trouble.

Our mothers are clever. They must realise how important it is to have exactly two pieces for everyone, and that's what they have given us. Even so, I come close to missing out because of the delay with Terry Taylor. I have to grab my second piece from Micky Marsline.

The referee is back in the middle of the field and blowing his whistle for the second half. John jumps up and down and yells out 'Get control, Den. Get control.'

I have switched wings. Mrs Costello has decided I will be better there, so I am still on the same side as the mothers.

John is right. We have no chance of ever getting the Miramar Inquisition going, and making the lives of all the Protestants a terrible misery, if we don't get control of the game. Nothing less than the future of religious hatred in Miramar is to be decided in the next twenty minutes. John knows this. He huddles next to Mum, looking anxious. This is the second time he has done this. I am going to have to talk to him about this. The monks who rampaged around Spain, terrifying and interrogating everyone, did not huddle up next to their mums!

We do much better in the second half. We pass the ball around a lot, and look good. The problem is that Terry Taylor and the rest of their backs have been listening to their coach and are stopping our attacks.

We are getting worried. We keep attacking and they keep defending. It is almost as if someone has written a script, with 1-0 to Miramar North as the final line. We have shots at goal. They go over the top, around the side or they get saved by their goalkeeper.

It is getting near the end of the game. The referee is starting to look at his watch. We need to score two goals right now if we are going to get a win. This isn't going to be easy. Terry Taylor is back in their defence and doing a brilliant job against us.

It's a horrible thought but I sense that Marist Miramar is in a dark, dark time. The future of the Under-11 Eastern Suburbs Wednesday league is hanging right here, and so is the Miramar Inquisition, and they are both close to death.

Somehow this sense of overwhelming panic completely misses the mothers. Instead of panic-driven screams demanding tactical shifts, there is stuff coming from the sidelines like, 'My youngest is walking now and I've got enough baby clothes to sink a ship. Why don't you come around tomorrow and have a look, and see if there is anything you can use.' Don't they know how important this game actually is?

The referee has another look at his watch. We are desperate on attack and the mothers are getting worse. 'Oh dear, our bring-and-buy is the same day! Why don't we join up and have a much bigger one? If that works, we can do something really spectacular next year!' Ye gods!

Suddenly there is a chance. Their fullback gives the ball a massive kick. It's supposed to go straight up the field, but instead it skids off the side of his boot and comes straight to me. I get to it and trap it and take off towards their goal. I go past one of their halves and then another. There is nothing ahead of me except their goalkeeper. Just as I am about to take the shot I hear Terry Taylor right beside me. 'I gotcha!' he gasps.

It takes only a second to see he may be right. The

angle I need to beat to get to the goal is getting tighter and tighter. So I stop and turn inside. Terry goes straight past. I fire it as hard as I can to Micky Marsline, who sticks his foot out. The ball hits it at the perfect spot and flies straight into the corner of their goal.

Terry Taylor and some of their players yell, 'Offside!'

The referee looks around. One of their fullbacks is sitting near the goal, doing up his bootlaces. He didn't see anything until we scored our goal, but he is there, and that means there are enough of their players between us and the Miramar North goal. The referee waves away the defender and blows his whistle for a goal. Terry Taylor is really, really, really unhappy looking. Great!

As we run back I ask the referee how long there is to go. 'Not long. Just get on with it!'

The mothers stop talking when they see the goal, and clap politely. Politely! Even Mrs Costello isn't yelling and screaming any more. This is awful. Surely the spirit of reconciliation between Catholics and Protestants isn't sweeping over her as well? Isn't there anything left sacred? When religious hatred fails what else is left?

Brother Brian has turned up, joining the mothers on the sidelines. I like that, because he has his huge, deep, powerful voice. It ought to be enough to frighten the life out of the Miramar North defence, long enough for us to slip past and score a winning goal. He lets out what I thought is a pretty sad little effort, 'Come on Marist.' Then he says to the mothers, 'There, I'm supposed to do that. And I did. Obligations done!' The mothers all laugh.

Miramar North kick off. We stop their attack near the top of our penalty area and begin coming back at them. I can feel my heart going at a million miles an hour. The referee looks at his watch again, and holds his whistle as if he is going to blast the end of the game.

Brother Brian is shaking hands with the mothers and congratulating them for getting the bring-and-buy organised. I think I even heard him offer to let Protestant kids practise with our softball team if they want!

One of the Protestant mothers says, 'Can I ask you something? It's a bit cheeky!'

Brother Brian smiles and nods.

'You're supposed to be celibate, aren't you? I don't suppose you want my husband for a recruit do you? He likes being celibate, too.'

Brother Brian says, 'It's official with me!' Everyone laughs, then he adds, 'The Lord moves in mysterious ways.'

The Protestant mother says, 'He doesn't move at all. That's the trouble!'

Hey! What about our game? It is the biggest moment in the season and all the mothers are hardly watching. Now our headmaster is no better. Whoops. I nearly miss the ball coming my way. It is a bad pass from one of their halves. I get it and start another dribbling run. Everyone is supposed to be watching me, but John tells me later, when I ask if the adults see my big moment, that they are busy organising meat packs for a combined rapid-raffle night.

Their defence is crowding in on me. The referee puts the whistle in his mouth. There is no time left for anything. I let fly, kicking the ball as hard as I can at their goal. It hits the top of Terry Taylor's head, and flies over their goalkeeper.

The ball zooms high in the air and drops down towards their goal. It looks as if I might have scored the winning goal, without properly realising it. I tell myself to wait until the ball goes in the goal before I do any leaping up and yelling and shouting and celebrating.

It is such a good shot it even stops the mothers from talking.

It hasn't gone in the net. It bounces on their crossbar and goes straight up in the air. If it lands on the other side it is a goal kick, which is no good to us. If it comes back on our side it might bounce where we can get another shot at it. Everyone is sprinting at it. Terry Taylor and I are side by side.

The ball drops back in the field. It hits the ground. It must have fallen on some sand or something because it doesn't bounce. It stops and then trickles towards the goal, and stops!

It is right on the line. Just sitting there.

I am just about to kick it in the goal. Terry Taylor is going to slide under my legs and flick it away. Then . . . the referee blows the whistle!

I get there first and the ball zooms into the goal.

The referee stands there smiling. 'Sorry, no goal. The whistle's gone.'

'Whadda ya mean, no goal!'

'The time is up and I blew the whistle. End of game. End of story.'

The referee isn't interested in our protests. He walks over to the sideline, goes up to Brother Brian and sticks his hand out. 'Jim Farquhar. I'm the Head here.'

'Brother Brian. Nice to meet you.'

'I thought a draw would be good.'

'Ideal,' answers Brother Brian.

It's all very well for them, smiling and chatting and deciding the right thing has been done. No one asks us. I still think this isn't much of a result at all.

The mothers all say goodbye to each other and promise to ring each other up with the arrangements for bring-and-buy sales.

John says, 'You were great.'

'Thanks, John. If you had played we would have won for certain.'

Terry Taylor is just behind us. 'Hard luck about you not getting the goal at the end,' he says.

We look around to see if his mother has forced him to say that. No, she hasn't. She is talking to some other mothers, miles away.

John and I look at each other. For a half second we are going to start the Miramar Inquisition and say something nasty to him. But he sticks out his hand. 'Shake?'

John and I look at each other again. If we shake his hand, that is the end of the Miramar Inquisition.

John pushes past and shakes, even though he is the one Terry beat up.

I am a bit ashamed about that, so I shake his hand too.

Our mums have been talking to each other. They

come over and round us up. Mum says, 'See, they can be friends if they try.'

Terry Taylor's mum puts her hand around his shoulder. 'It's not that difficult when you put your mind to it.'

'No, Mum,' he mutters.

They go off to their car. John and Mum and I go off to the Ford Popular. As we pass the headmaster's office, I hear Jim Farquhar saying, 'Whisky?'

'Don't mind if I do.'

'What exactly do I call you — Father or Brother?'

'Brian's fine.'

'Do you want water with it?'

'Good God!'

'Sorry.'

'Bottoms up!'

We had many games after that, but no more religious hatred stuff was in any of them. If there was a moment when the Catholic ghetto ended, at least for two soccer teams of eight and nine-year-olds this was it.

But on the day itself, I don't care. John and I are in a hurry to get home, so we can play the match all over again on our back lawn. Only this time there isn't going to be any blowing whistles to make sure the game ends in a draw. We will play until we have a winner.

That means a game to the death, or until our dad comes home and we get called in for dinner.

The End